DarkHart Writings:

Bloody Endurance
Chronicles of an Endurance Warrior

By
Endurance Warrior

TABLE OF CONTENTS:

Acknowledgements

Thank you to my parents for their unconditional love and support through all of the past, present, and future struggles. Thanks to all of my friends, near or far, who have been there for me and hold me up through their prayers. Thank you, Katie, for first encouraging me to put pen to paper in the dark times, and for inspiring me with your own writings. Most of all, thanks be to God; Jesus, our Lord and Savior. Thank You for your sacrifice, Your unconditional love and mercies, and for Your provision and protection throughout my life. I would also like to thank each artist that generously allowed me to feature their art alongside each poem:

Obliterate Oblivion

Ascary Lazos (Hikaruga)

EiMoOo (cover art)

Breakerr

Dani-Owergoor

AnonymousToStrangers

Pure-Poison89

Anthony-G

FallanDark

Suntwirl

MagicsArt

Blue-a

IrvingGFM

Blaithiel

BigBad-Red

DiosaEMR

Berryblu

Palantirs (pg. 1 "The Silence of the Roses" http://palantirs.deviantart.com/)

Barbara Florczyk (Kokoszkaa)

ErikShoemaker

NeverDying

Each of these artists' complete works can be found at
www.Deviantart.com. *Their specific links can be found*
captioned underneath each of their works throughout the
book.

EXPRESSIONS OF AGONY

Schrei II by Obliterate Oblivion-

http://obliterateoblivion.deviantart.com/gallery/

I was placed in this world of distress

Called forth out of the nothingness

But forced in like the rat in a maze

Audienced by malevolent spectators all of my days

Born into a role I wished not portray

Pushed into games I don't want to play

Bound and ever paralyzed by Terrors-

Never to speak that I may

Be pulled into the violent light of each day

Mind darkened, body dead inside

But who is to blame?

In whom shall I confide?

Perished within

So young to be one with Death

Like living deceased

Before ever even finding my breath

I hunger not, thirst not, yearn for nothing less

Than the relief of Agony's final kiss

Yet he evades me, tormenting day and night

Awake or asleep, he mocks my inner plight

Yet an unforeseen force preserves my breath

But only enough to expand this chest

Only enough air to maintain the pain

Giving only enough strength to be able of suffering

Trapped inside this vessel

Cage of thorns inside

Pierced and sinking deeper

Spectators look and chide

Gored upon its savage claws

Glistening scarlet ribbons encircling each wrist:

The only evidence of a steel affair's solace:

Crying out for Death's wicked embrace

For Darkness' security

Seeking the Taskmaster's satiety

And Suffering's surety

The Legion shrouds my head

Demons crowd about my bed

Watching whilst I sleep

Afflicting me with dreams

Wrapping their hands around my neck

So none can hear me scream

In daytime gnawing, whispering, and condemning at my ear

So long in Agony's grasp, lights extinguished by the care

Of devastated lands; this world's imminent despair

I see through iris engulfed by black

And hear only lament

But no longer do I fear inside their malicious intent

You can see why in my eyes

Where darkness deeper than thine lies

Hardened by the years at Agony's hands

It consumes you

Growing.

Feeding.

On the best years of toil your body can give

Upon all the fear, hate, abandonment through which one can live

The bitter seed choking its recipient from within

Stretching, squeezing

Breaking out through all the smiles faked

Yet captured in the image by which I've been forsaken

If it shall make me suffer, so shall I to it

Demons enter into flesh through these open wrists

Tearing me apart from the inside out

It will all end up in blood for blood

Without a single doubt

How long must I bear this body of death

While Hope has forgotten me

While Love has fled my presence

And faith been suffocating?

Will Agony just let go of me?

Will the Son ever shine on me again?

Where can I hide...where can I hide?

Where is my Savior, Lord, my friend?

Puppet

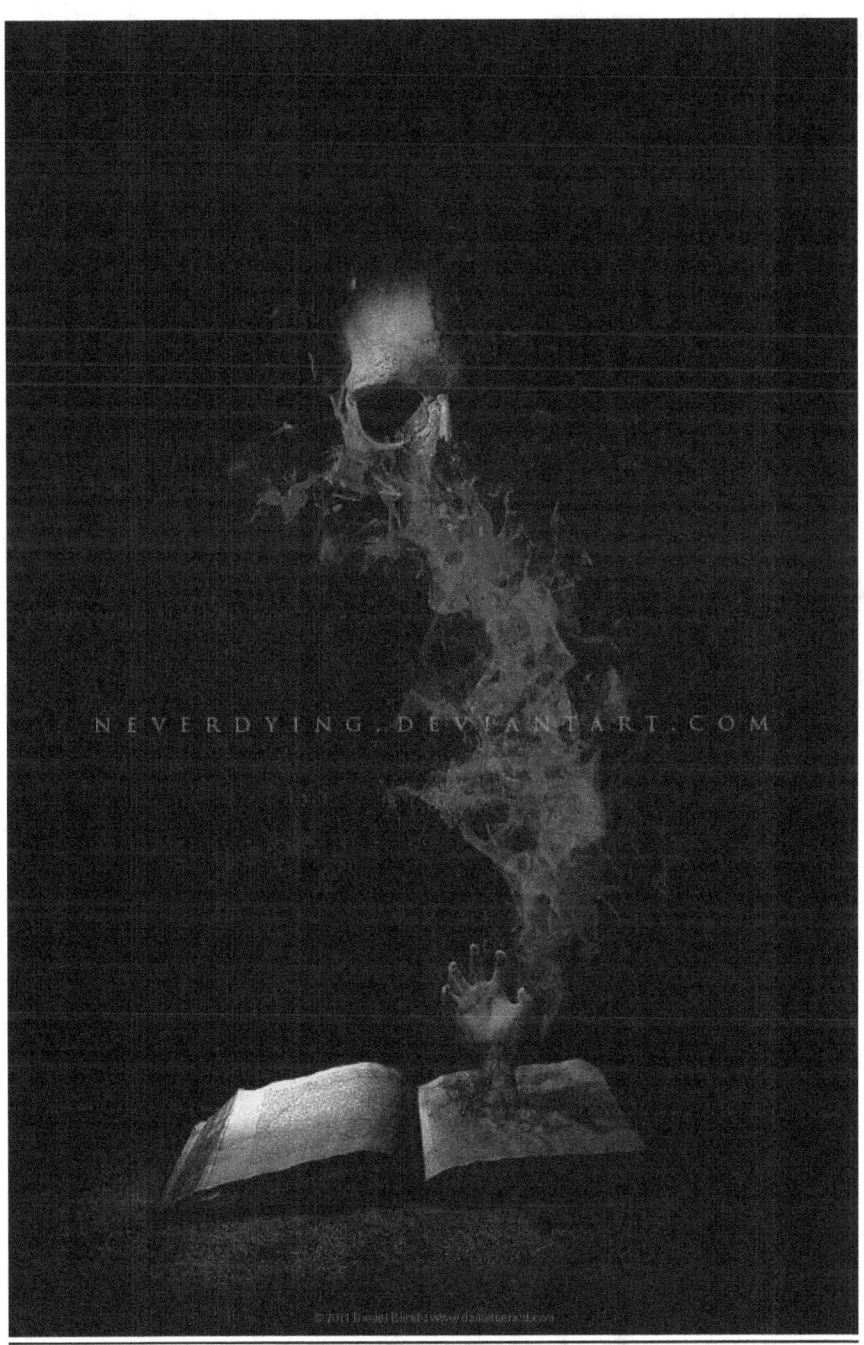

The Wishmaster by NeverDying-http://neverdying.deviantart.com/

I tire of doing all these things

Day after day, it's mind numbing

Sucking the life right out of your soul

Ever consuming, a great black hole

I try and do all these things for myself

Hoping one day to achieve health or wealth

But as soon as it's done-
It all becomes UN

Just as I reach-
Only more trial has my soul to teach

Right as any strength can finally be found

Creation all hurries back into the ground

I toil to make for myself a place

As soon as it's seen, more Anguish seeks my face

Ever before God, making its case

TIME'S RITUAL

Too Much by EiMoOo- www.EiMoOo.DeviantArt.com

I just wanna quit

I don't want to do it!

This tiresome ritual that comes day after day

Another meal to eat, hour to age, another bill to pay

Mankind sentenced to fight

But Time will always have its way

Struggle though you may-

It pushes and pulls you forward until you are broken and

gray

Locked inside the travesty

Feel in your bones the minutes go by

Tick- tock sounds the clock

How many more 'til you die?

I just don't want to do it!

This paying for air...

Step outside the trap if you dare

From school to school to job to career:

I never could manage to feign that I cared

Present never satisfies, future fills me with fear

Past unrelenting until I can't hear

But my own small, pathetic whimper, falling on deaf ears

What sickness constrains me, that I cannot get up-

Before I've no more years?

Pleading it be sent out, rather than erased

To wander the Earth; empty souls to be chased

Now tidied and swept clean, delivered from Hate

Better find fast with what you'll fill that space

Hesitate too long and they'll find you again

More evil than before, and now It's brought friends

Thrice the trouble your eyes shall they see

For now you're just a vessel

The puppet of Agony's

ONCE AGAIN

Here I am

Once Again

Another six months down the line…

Not even in the same place, but only further behind

As I lay here in the old familiar spot,

It gnaws ruthlessly at my mind

All my planning, all my striving, all my pointed strategizing-

FAILED.

Once again

Another hunk Agony's torn away from my soul

Can there ever be a Once Again whole?

I've gotten nowhere, but have to Once Again try

Despite the discouraged cry of everything inside

Once Again

 I won't just lie down and die

Endlessly the daylight drags on and on

With another war to fight

Once Again

I'm holding on- tired and worn; anticipating the night

I can't surrender in the light of day

Though I don't know how long I can carry on this way

But this Sun never sets, there are no stars to guide

No Moon ever shines, permitting to rest inside

The Enemy never lays his weapons down and will never run

Not before the setting of an everlasting Sun

Once Again

My strength worn thin

In this brutal war of attrition

How long until God will hear my petitions?

If not - I simply must give in

For the victor declared, it's already been

And I've already lost

Once Again.

TARGET POINT

Post Mortem Passion by Breakerr- http://breakerr.deviantart.com/gallery/

I won't just settle, not until I'm dead

I will not inherit the truth of lies within your head

I won't be like you: victimized by the years gone by

Stand up from underneath the yoke!

You declared defeat, but didn't even try!

Fight for change, take back some control!

Stop submitting to the swift fall of it all!

Everything's breaking down, we can both see

More gravity, more struggle, more adversity

Call forth more might, more life, more fight!

Grow, resurrect failed strength

Continue to walk this night!

Never relent, never bow down!

Take It out before It puts you in the ground!

Merciless intentions it's got out for you

In ruthless pursuit, reciprocate it too!

Get up! Get out of self pity!

For there will be no sympathy

Agony and all his friends don't eat, won't sleep

Bent to separate soul from spirit

So recompense for all the tears shed

For the target is now upon YOUR head.

SLAVE TO THE GRAVE

No matter how much pain, it won't quench my own disdain

A big ugly mar; I can't wash away this stain

The inferior exterior feeling that I hold in vain

This insanity of vanities, but I cannot get away

All these things I hate overtake

And cannot seem to ever be sated

Never before have I been in this place

Or ever before felt so powerless

Every identity I've sought been erased

Each dream I'd only seen, begging to be chased

Double- minded, tossed about on waves of the sea

Dying to fold into the mold I've felt I should be

Live to play upon the ledge

Only to push it over the edge

Constantly abusing this body just to exhaust negative energy

Push and push to suck it dry

Only feeding the need to bleed

Sitting in this skin is akin

To wearing a giant imposition

Yet perfection is only a fleeting apparition

Fruitless endeavor!

A chasing after the wind!

Screams my intuition

Yet like a net it baits and pulls me in

Time and time and time again

But I don't want to be a slave to the grave

I long to flee its presence, break these chains, be free!

But Oh my sweet Addiction, *don't let go of me!*

PLEAD TO THE HIGHEST

Hope by Dani- Owergoor: http://dani-owergoor.deviantart.com/

God on high, please forgive me

But I have to ask You…

I know I'm just another of millions

Who have dared to question Your truth

It's not that I'm asking for Your existence's proof

But are You ever going to see me through?

Please, just one little sign that You even hear me

All of my screaming

Or catch even just the scent of my bleeding

I've been asking, begging, praying, seeking

Release from this body of Death

Of pain, Depravity, torment, and reeking

Wound from the thorn that's been placed in my flesh

I find no escape by sleep; my bloodshot eyes find no rest

Fears and Terrors tear me apart night and day

I reach for companionship, but my demons scare them away

Who else can know the depths of my despair?

Please, just a little sign that You're still there

That You actually care

Or You'll cease just watching the falling of my tears

8 years and no light I've yet known

Since then darkness has only grown

No end to this night

Could only forceful death be the end of this plight?

You made this and every universe, but still

Won't touch this infection poised to kill

Or heal the inside of a soul

Dying only to be whole

FAKE PATHS

Another day has passed in a blur

What was accomplished? I'm never sure

I'm here at the end of it, bed soaked with tears

Just like the countless others that have made up my years

When will I finally live?

When did my best become inadequate to give?

Where lay my purpose, the path out of this void

Companions who once cared, only left annoyed

I've searched, sought, and struggled

But everything's still falling all around

Desperately I cup the blood spilled up off the ground-

And I'm left with searing emptiness.

I'm getting better at faking it now-

Growing in strength and looking more tough

But silently hope

For a way to fix it up!

The world really thinks I'm all better; that I'm happy

They base their assumptions on that seen outwardly; cowardly.

No matter how far I wander or how long I run

I'm wounded,

Running on fumes of adrenaline ; it is never done

Unfortunately, it's a race that can never be won

This facade that I wear for myself and the world

Has run its course

Tattered and torn, it won't last any more

Always stripped from me, passing the threshold of my door

Who knows the number of my tears that wash the floor?

Who sees?

Who can comfort me?

Don't know how long I can numb and distract myself out here

It's only a matter of **when,** I fear

That the winds shall blow icy

These paths be lonely

These hills will be silent - the heights and I only

What of the day that my strength finally fails?

Who will rescue me?

From where then shall my help be?

But as for tonight, I can only weep.

TAKE IT AWAY

Hope by Dani Owergoor-

http://dani-owergoor.deviantart.com/

What I wouldn't give to live in yesterday

The only time that I know it all turns out okay

Dear Holy Spirit, give me the strength for one more day

Oh Holy Father, let there be mercy over me

Jesus continue to petition that I may see

I was made for so much more than this

Meant to seek, serve, and glorify Thee

To one day walk beside You, apart from Depravity

I've been worn to the bone dry

All out of plans to try

Hardly the life of spirit left to write this line

Mind running blank, retreating inside

Like another part of me has started to die

Lord, You of all can see that I'm all out of fight

My soul has wandered aimlessly throughout each night

Never catching its breath or finding its rest

The burdens upon threaten to crush in this chest

I need Your help now, more than I've ever known…

BUT I JUST CAN'T SEEM TO COME ON MY OWN!

I need You to defend me, to fight for me here

Take it away!

For I can no longer stand against Fear

SUBCONSCIOUS MEMORIES

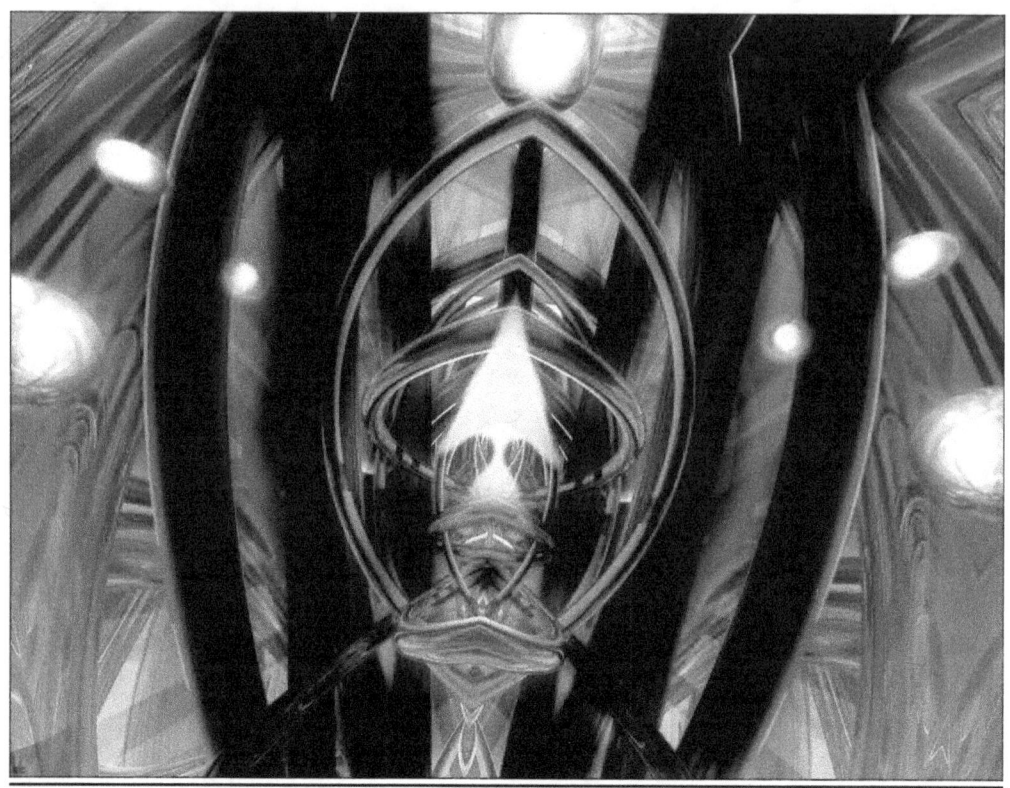

Mon Diable Synthetique by AnonymousToStrangers-
http://anonymoustostrangers.deviantart.com/

Get it out!

Out of my mind, these taunting confines

What I want so badly to say
But am unable to find the way

I can't pull it in nor push it away

Something inside I can't identify

It won't be ignored

Yet cannot be explored

I try and contrive the means to reset

But I can't be distracted, nor can I forget!

Ever before me, an inch out of reach

When I turn to face, it takes one step away

Choose to give chase, it becomes then evasive

Whispering, whispering now at my ear

"You call me, then run. But now I am here!"

Turn my back again; I still can sense its leer

Get it off!

When I feel its embrace

Get it out!

But then, "Why can't you stay?"

I can't have you, but you're always in sight

Then leave me alone! At least for a night

I can't get a grip on it, nor push it away

Try to sleep it all off, but it's there the next day

Half hoping, half not, I'll find you as I rise

"I've had enough!"

But still get lost within your eyes

Mesmerized

Hypnotized

Defenseless

A fool for fantasizing

Weaving throughout

Crawling within

Inhabiting my dreams

Filling me up with

Subconscious Memories

Like the person you love, but never have met

Even if come morning, the details I forget

Plain as the writhing in my gut

I swear

Its mark is still upon me

I know You were there.

But again seek after You,

I never would dare

Something new stirring deep within

Burning and calling, enticing me in

But it only leads in circles, for You drip with poison

I cannot reject you, thou knowest all too well

Leading me down to my own personal hell

I can't get a grasp of it nor let it go away

Let me alone or I'll surely go insane!

I can't get a hold of you nor throw you away

Get out! Leave me alone!

If You won't come to stay

NO LONGER

It's no longer safe to say

That you'll never feel a certain way

Push to put it out of mind

But safety never existed anyway, outside the house of the

Divine

But your eyes shall see the day

Your thoughts will lead you like a slave

These thoughts that dictate what we say

Also go astray

Dragging you around where you do not want to go

Teaching you the feelings that you did not wish to know

And who then knows the way back?

No, it's no longer safe to say

That I'll never feel a certain way

That I'll never feel that person's pain

or another human's sick disdain

My eyes will not shut tonight

My mind no rest resume

Until I can explain

that never again will I assume:

I cannot feel a certain way

No struggle or torment is below me

For to live is to suffer this ongoing Depravity

Bearing with one another is the only way that we can be

No longer slaves to the loss of sympathy

I'm being forced to understand

That which I never would have planned-

That which I never would have wanted.

But nothing's out of the question now

Just a matter of when I'll get back to sleep

And try to forget somehow.

DEAR FEAR

Dear Fear,

I just wanted to say

That I'll always still be here

You forget all the years I've spent all alone

In the winter's chill, summoning the strength to fight on my own

I will wield all the weapons that I have honed

Utilize all the fury to justice that have been sown

And you'll feel all the terrors that you have bestowed

I'll lay you to the grave, 'til you're no longer known

I'll turn back against you all of this anger

Digging it deeper 'til you're just a stranger

No matter how much pain

I've been myself more fiercely trained

Brought myself up just as unfeeling

For you, my enemy: just as unyielding

This is my war cry

Through **Bloody Endurance** !

I'm making use of my time

For I know that I shall never die

Taking back all you have stolen

I claim it for my own

Even though this Earth is really not my home

Fear, your condemnation alone then shall you hear

For your own end, draws more clear and near

So live out the length of your days

And you'll do your best to oppress

Then on That Day, you will pass away

But I will be here still

And forever here to stay.

<u>BLEED</u>

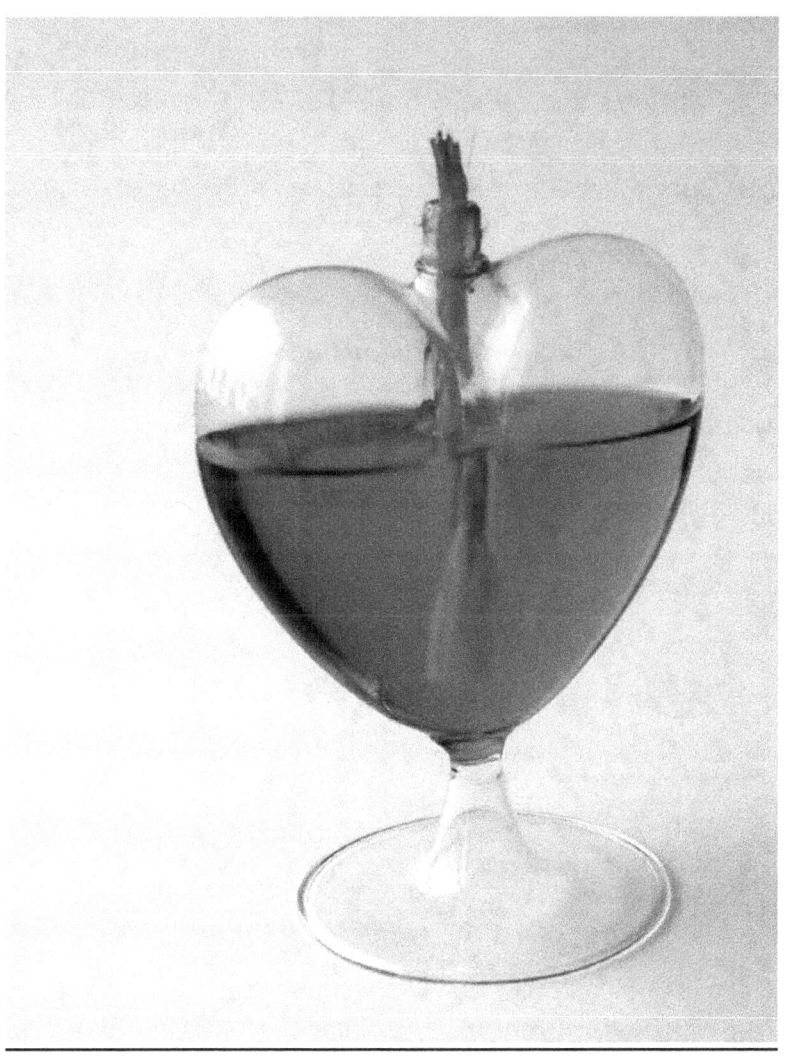

I can't believe you'd betray me like this

Luring me in with the venomous kiss

I've been here before again and again

But had hoped we'd moved on

That I'd call you my friend

I've walked how you said

Through where you forced me in

And it all fell apart, not even just the same

But worse than before…

NO MORE OF THIS GAME!

Remember I said I'd never do this again

I won't look back

Because you just won't understand

I thought I'd bled enough for you…

Offering me your hand

You'll again watch me be torn open

But not in the way you had planned

I wish I could dissociate

Putting aside the misunderstanding

Which separates us, ever living

Wish I could push away the hatred that burns

As you say it's only out of concern

I thought I'd bled enough for you...

That you'd never again put me through

The mechanism that broke me

Into more than just two

Ripping apart

Pieces precariously taped together

From long before the start

You think you know better and what's best for me

But as blind as I am, you equally won't see

That I've truly no more blood to give...

Exhausted everything, just trying to live

Trapped in my mind's own prison

You say I want to dwell here

But to my ear, that's derision!

If just for a second you saw through my vision

Felt for a moment the searing incision

In body and mind-

You'd see that it's not a decision

No, none could count the tries that I've given

Who can measure the sorrow

I've endured yesterday, today, and tomorrow?

If I could have chosen another fate

I'd have taken the easy way

And even if I may hold the keys

To the locks inside of me

I've nothing left to bleed...

Naught to put my mind at ease

GO AHEAD

<u>Save My Broken Heart</u> by Pure-Poison89-

<u>http://pure-poison89.deviantart.com/</u>

And so it begins

This war, neither of us shall bow in

Go Ahead

Do what you can to add to my Agony

Making your new little rules to spite me

And we'll begin all over again

Just like when I was only ten

Go Ahead

Keep the back door in check

And put your leash back around my neck

But can you really hold it?

It's all fine with me, there's nothing left to see

Go Ahead

Suck me dry again, all the life left in me

You won't get any more, there's nothing left to bleed.

And I'll hide myself away

In the last sacred place

Lock it all up in a box

Smash in the locks

And swallow the key

Go Ahead

Make it your point to torment me

Surely I've not suffered enough!

So Go Ahead

Do as you must!

SHEOL'S SOULS

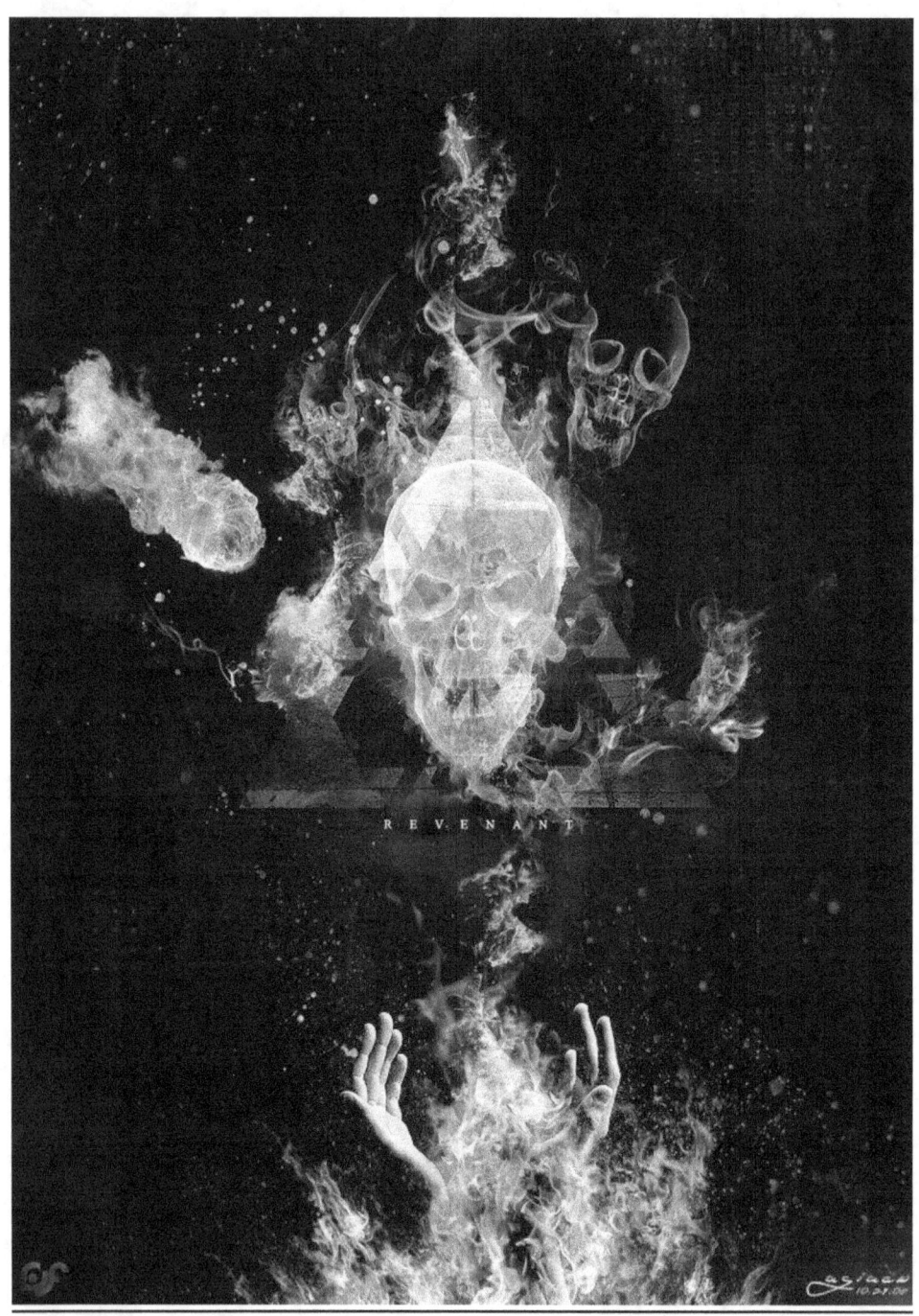

Revenant by Anthony-G- http://anthony-g.deviantart.com/

I know the path that I would take

If God I ever were to forsake

I feel the way that I would go

In my flesh, what no one else knows

All the good in me is not my own

For I died within so long ago

Gave away my spirit and soul

Couldn't hold on, no longer whole

I'll give you these pieces

But the rest has already been sold

Enslaved and ransomed

Temptation takes its toll

We've all cheapened ourselves

Sold out to Depravity

Though made to walk in sacred Peace

Will I choose the noose

Or flee into deserts dry

Run right off the cliffs

Trusting I survive

Or that on wings of an eagle, I would learn to fly?

Oh Father, don't let go of me

Chain me at Your feet if need be

If to preserve my soul!

Don't let me walk into the hole

down into the grave, to join **Sheol**!

I will never fathom or discern God's ways

Why He lets us burn and learn

In this world, just to find our place

And then, so brief a stay

Before our tracks are forever erased

Gone, as soon as we find that easy pace

After the **Winds** we ever will be chasing

But we can't stop now

The universe requires somehow

Us, made out of the dust

Back to which we will rest

During the time allotted to you

Now is the time for you to choose

Through fear and agonizing:

You can reject or submit to the Power that's higher

But to where will your spirit go when you finally expire?

I WEPT

Now It's Just Me and Lonliness- by FallanDark-
http://fallandark.deviantart.com/

I wept and wept and wept

Fearing alone that I would not be kept

I said "I am Jonah, created for Your service

If I truly am running away from Your wish

Right now Lord God, send out the fish!

To take me to Nineveh, the place that I hate"

I screamed "chain me at Your feet!

That I not gain the world and lose my own soul!"

I pleaded "Place in my chest just the one breath to say yes!

If this IS Your will, if this is Your best..."

I wept and wept and wept

Fearing alone that I would not be kept

Cut myself open, seeking the strength to accept

Screaming and writhing on the ground

Prostrated and waiting to be bound

Listening and dreading the War Horn's familiar sound-

But it never resounded.

Still I wept and wept and wept

Fearing alone that I would not be kept

Not for fearing I was doing the wrong thing

But that I'd be again thrown away

That you'd perceive it as a betrayal

Because our fates do not all resolve in the same way

My path is not over, but I am still here to stay

And on that same road

I met one I loved, though just barely know

Believe me or not, a different way must I go

This is NOT my retreat

I do NOT admit defeat

Though you may not agree, or differently see

My soul hopes you'll call me friend

In more than just my memories again

LEAVE

I don't know I'll be able to find the words this time

To come up with more breaths set in rhymes

Filled only with words too weak to convey

What I feel inside, for they've lost use this day

Used for hypocrisy and tearing down

Only good for breaking, for tossing around

I'm all used up, just leave me alone!

I don't want to talk

Despite your polite knock

I'm all worn out, just leave me alone

I don't want to relate

Disappointment only yesterday

I need time to again relearn this circuitry

To recharge and rewire

Just leave me alone

Cuz I'm all out of fire

I don't want to connect

Give me my time to weep and reflect

But torturously more is continually demanded

No time to heal from constant reprimanding

Just go away and leave me alone!

To sit amidst the silence

And save you from my violence

Soon I'll take my hands to rebuild

Refill the capacity of my will

Try to again find those words to say-

BUT NOT TODAY

I'm no good this way…

Leave me alone…just go away…

But I'm still stuck here in front of you

With nothing left to say…

TIDE'S TIME

Beyond the Sea III by Dani Owergoor-

http://dani-owergoor.deviantart.com/

My entire life I have feared

The excruciatingly perfect Storm

And now It is here.

I couldn't have fathomed such high waves

Threatening to pull me down to the grave

I can't force the tide
But neither can I hide

Though I keep my hands to the sail
My strength is all to no avail
I open my mouth to pray
But the tears fill my lungs ; no words to say

I'd never have imagined so treacherous a Beast at sea
Hunting and churning these waters for me
It's bounty's been placed upon my head
Lying in wait for me to be dead

But I can't turn the tide
Nor can I hide

Passing over these waters

Doom gnawing at my mind

All the distance that I've covered, silently passing behind

It would all amount to nothing

If this is how I'm dying.

But these hands shall keep fast

Clutched to the mast

Though outside of my control

My fate has now been cast

All that I could do has already been done

And on this final night, there's nowhere left to run

I thought I would escape

For I made it all this way

But I can't turn back time

No, I cannot fix mistakes

I can't turn this tide

-Nowhere to hide.

I rise and turn to face It

Or It ever will be chasing

If It doesn't drag me down to Hell

It will indeed be a great tale to tell

But no time left for surmising

For the Beast is arising!

IT BEATS

Hope deferred makes the heart sick

But surely it can fail with enough of it

Once had its fill of Agony, Fear, Depravity

But on it beats and beats and beats

I don't want it anymore- this burden to feel so deeply

To experience the abysmal depths of each suffering

To be Pain's closest friend, Darkness' most intimate lover

Surely my time has passed and you can find another?

Where is the way out of this deadly contract?

All I've gained is a toxic dose of aggression

But starting in again- frustrated tears of depression

Not enough- words, tears, blood- not enough for expression

What makes this heart beat and beat and beat

I've tried to make it stop

While other organs fail so easily

Ears ringing from chaos

Kidneys strained from distress

Liver backed up from stress

To the pit of my stomach

Every affliction causes inconsistence

But heart persists- it beats and beat and beats

Long after the mind has made its last retreat

Wish I could just cut my heart out sometimes

And silence all of its murderous lies

No longer have to remember, mourn, miss, measure, regret

I just need some peace inside; I just want to forget!

But the heart is desperately wicked, who can know it?

Yeah, I'd lock it in a box for a while

So I can finally pretend and put on a smile

I could take my place in the parade of happy faces

"Fake it 'til you make it!"

But I suck at make believe

I know you're sick of hearing it- these lines of misery...

As only few of us walk their jagged roads to destiny

But with all this pain I pray

I pave a path for the next soul sentenced to go this way

So they can know- though they too are alone

Another was here, who too stumbled through

By just another beat and beat and beat...

WHO I WAS

I'm not who I was-

That girl you thought you knew

Once so full of life, energy, and jokes

Pretty little thing; holding faith, love, and hope

All that was left in your memory when you walked away so

long ago

Anywhere In time's landscape, near or far

Regardless of who you were, who you are

I'm not who I was anymore.

No, that girl's gone.

Sure, I remember her too

So strong, faithful, bold, and clear

The Sovereign's voice her highest call

Running and seeking, didn't even see my own fall

What happened to it all?

Don't know that today I'd be able to look her in the eyes

As it turns out I couldn't even walk my own advice

Cuz I'm not who I was.

And as cliché as it may sound...

I don't even know who I am.

All I can understand

Is that I'm no longer that girl, so innocent and pure

But lain with Darkness, tasting bitter

I don't know me anymore

If I even yearn to be what I was before

But wondering, always wondering

Will I be here forever, will I ever be found?

But who's even to come around

None to love- who could love me?

No, nothing but to remember who I was; and they sit
contentedly

And nothing for me but to be haunted by the memories

In my dreams,

Who was there,

For whom I cared,

Who I was,

Who I no longer can be.

Replaying, reliving, dripping with regret in my mind

But again I claim I can't turn back time

And as you come and go again, I just had to let you know

I'm not who I was

And we have to let her go.

ONE NIGHT IN MY NIGHTMARES

Amongst a large company of beings

Crowded in a small, dimly lit room

Each draped with inexplicable darkness

I am one too.

A room full of souls, but silence hangs thick in the air

Only then a murmur of small talk, a feigning to care

All need to feed

Yet some can still also bleed

The nonsense dies down

One slumps to the ground

Two others follow suit, making hardly a sound

Sparking each shadow to erupt into chaos

All morbid stillness thrown off and lost

The thirst sets in

And all tear limb from limb

Friends turned to foe

My pupils start to grow

Restraining

Containing

Amidst the violent show

Realization of betrayal

The Bloodship has failed.

I won't take the breath I labored to make

Nor destroy the lives I gave all to save!

Though all others gave in to the mind of Depraved

GET OUT NOW!

FIND A WAY SOMEHOW!

I flee through a door

Assault echoing down the corridor

But out sped by my own kind

Reality of second death laid to my mind

Hemmed in left and right

Before and behind, only left to fight

Now, I must be unrepressed on this night

Finally, I exonerate myself:

Spilling the blood of the damned, of whom I had once held hope.

Making path to the next room, I barricade myself in

Then lifting up a floorboard to lie in the small space within

Praying to the God I beg will recompense our sins

"Don't let them find me, save my wicked soul, seeking repentance"

But Hell will now have another admittance

For in the killers' grasp lay no room for forgiveness-

I have been found

My former fellow fiend drives a stake into the ground

Piercing through heart, my blood pooling all around

Their thirst sets in

And those I once called kin

Now tear me too limb from limb

But I cannot die

This night's walk never ends

As I stand again to rise

Knowing I must finish the very last of them

Lie in wait and find a way to put this to its end

Maniacal screams reverberate throughout the halls

Then I know I must another soul sadly bring its fall...

THE CULMINATION

Today I stumble through the Darkness' kingdom

Praying to trade in these scars one day for Wisdom

That all my pain will not be in vain

Perhaps somewhere along the way

I'll find some Happy and bring it with me

But it was well stated:

"Life is a path, death the destination!"

I know there will ultimately be the Culmination

Just as a huge collage
The final picture revealed
Beautifully composed

Of every Haunting Memory
All the torment of Depravity
And seemingly purposeless Agony

All Fear will disappear
Nightmares be dissolved
All will be seen in its eternal resolve

When we die, finally coming alive
And cross the veil that was torn
By He who wore the crown of thorns
Who parted with the Divine
So He could lay down His life- for mine

And I know He understands my pain

For Jesus tasted every form of suffering

Then resurrected from the dead

And ascended again

Each day He sympathizes patiently

Justifying, constantly interceding

I can only wait and pray until I'm shown

When by God's strength alone

He'll turn these rags to riches

To cast before His throne

WINDS

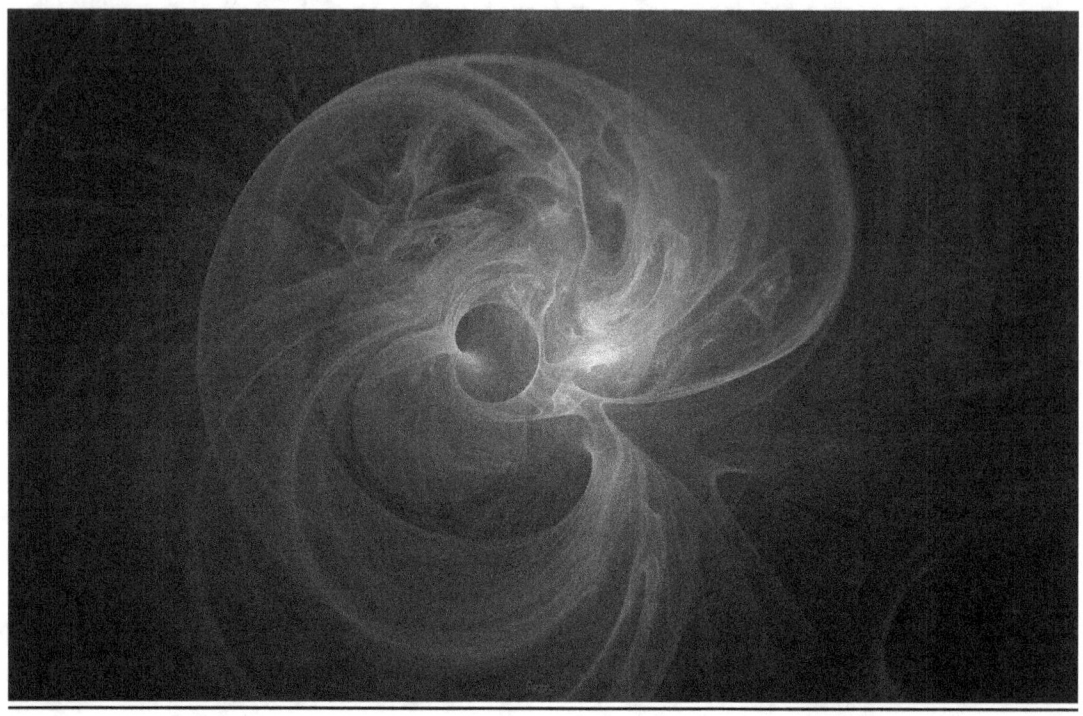

_X12080310_ by Hikaruga

In running the race appointed to me

I've been keeping with the Wind's pace

Still moving forward,

But slowing these days.

Stumbling

Tripping

Directionless.

Wondering at the moment
Where's gone succinct expression?

Left with nothing but the hollow aggression
Of chasing after the Winds
Starting in again- frustrated tears of depression

All continues in endless motion
The Winds work up again
Sweeping away the last of my devotion

Leaving unmotivation,
Desensitization,
Void of my own representation

"MEANINGLESS. MEANINGLESS."
The Winds whisper to my soul
Along this black hole through which I crawl
No doors, no windows, no walls

No, nothing to be seen at all

Just the Winds,

Endless echoes of its taunting call

SIMPLE

I wrote a little rhyme

That'll take only a moment of your time

Capture your short attention

So rise, learn, and gain real perception

To think above the elementary thoughts of today

Kudos to you... you understand the Simple's ways

As though it hadn't already been laid out plain as day

By the generations' repetitious mistakes

"When I was a child, I thought as a child"

So let us put away childish ways

Leave the obvious things unspoken

And let's learn a new way

WOUNDS- I WISH

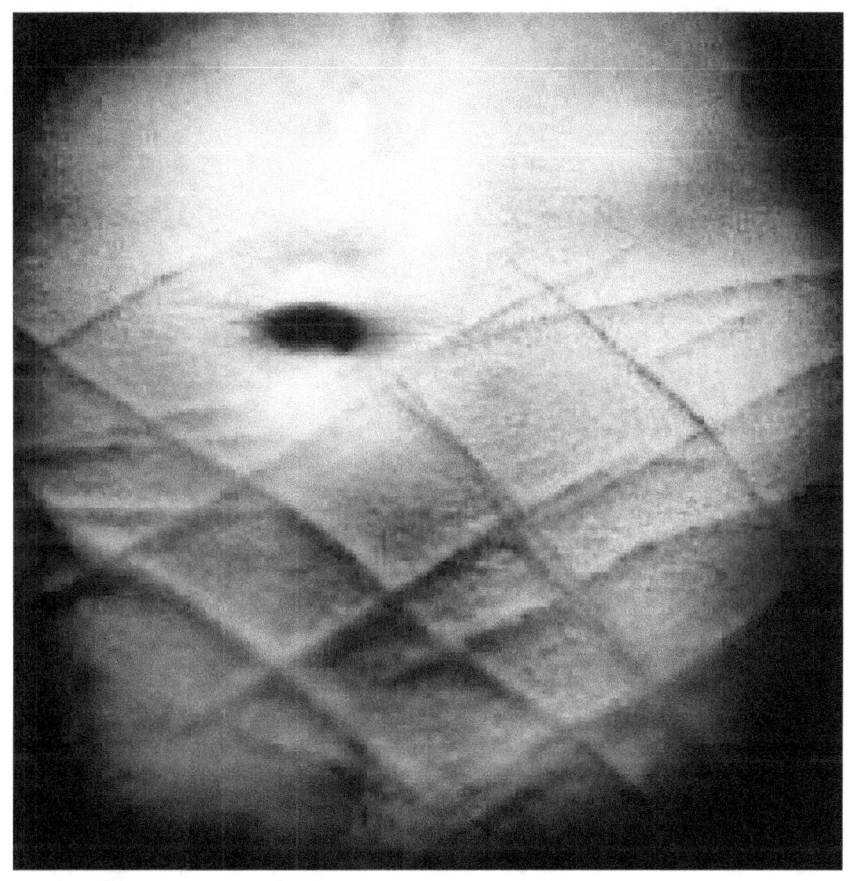

I wish I were free to live

That I had any love to give

I wish these wounds didn't bleed at every hour of the day

Wounds which wish that my injury…

Hurt only as much as the kind you can see

I wish I could even be set free

That there was ever a lock to this key

I wish I were the person I was

When you first met me

Yet I fear these demons constantly following

Will tear us both apart

When it was only my head they wanted

From the very beginning

When they first told me

They wouldn't rest until I laid in the grave

So you have to see...

I can never set down my weaponry

Where is my moment's rest?

I've had none, my soul can attest

I wish ease were as easy for me

That for a moment I could breathe

And really believe...

In happy endings

And that there's one out there for me.

.

THIS IS ME

V For Vampire by MagicsArt- http://magicsart.deviantart.com/gallery/

This is me

Not the nice time you thought I would be

This is me

Depressed and Depraved
Not the fun game that you'd wanna play

Yeah, this is me

I'm mostly black and grays
Haunted, tormented all of my days

This is me

Tired and torn
Shame and scorn
A **Slave to the Grave**

Yes, this is my Thorn

Darkened mind,

Porcupine,
Agonizing whirlwind inside

So this is me

Don't know what else there is to see
Cuz I haven't turned out
Who I was working to be

PEACE IN DEATH

<u>Fields of Gold</u> by Dani- Owergoor: <u>http://dani-owergoor.deviantart.com/</u>

It takes courage not to die, but to live

And with every passing season

Figuring out the reasons why

In Peace, you're not afraid to die

Weaved throughout this unfinished portrait

I can't wait to see the other side!

PRAYER OF PSALMS 6

My God, who is Love and slow to anger

Deliver me from my very soul's danger

But If You are displeased

Please be gentle with me

Upon these fragile, dry bones...

Shower your abundant mercies

Consider just how weak am I

...And heal me

Spirit and body

Troubles greatly torment these

For Your Name's sake only:

Deliver me!

For in the grave, I could give You no praise

Nor ever again lift up my voice to pray

I'm aging from grief - wasting away!

Every night sleepless, I call out to You

How Long, O Lord?

How long until You bring me through?

THE WAY THAT IT GOES

Friends Forever by Blue-a: _http://blue-a.deviantart.com/gallery/_

Despite my bitterness that overflows

This I know:

This is the way that it goes.

That it's only a matter of time

Until I can no longer kick against the goads

Despite my deepest inner beings' resistance

This is the way that it goes.

I just want to believe...

That though I feel alone

In a type of torment no one may so well know

Perhaps at least one other

Hates the way it goes.

Just one other single haunted soul

Who too sleeps on and walks upon

Similar burning coals

To bring two tortured hands to take hold

Suffer with one another

And let go-

Of being perfectly whole

DEEP INSIDE

October 2012 by _IrvingGFM- http://irvinggfm.deviantart.com/_

To yearn for it so deeply

To let it overtake me

Allow Darkness to consume completely

It would only be so easy!

It's my Kryptonite

Cyanide

Paralyzed and agonizing
Practicing at fantasizing

Why tears be my food and drink
What is it that you think?

Just to put it out there
Give credence to all who despair
Look upon if you dare-

Suicide.

Deep inside

I refuse to any longer hide

It stares at me all day and night
All my life I've had to fight
Resisting its seductive entice

Yet there lay no sleep in Death

For it is not the end

Its only waking up

For eternity to begin

And to those who choose

To take mortality into their own hand

Be no rest, but judgment

Nowhere to lay thy head

And so I'll suffer one more day

Though I wish that I were dead

TRAPPED

Let me out! Get me out!

Can't breathe, can't relax

Eye's iris ever engulfed by black

Adrenaline constantly pumping within

Better watch your back

For It's watching too

And forever pursuing Its sole victim- YOU

Darkness and Doom

Feeding on you

Lying in wait to shroud all with gloom

And gnawing-

Right at the base of your skull

Where Its home It's decided to call

Breathing, whispering at the back of your neck

Never permitting a moment of rest

Scraping down the spine

Whose plight you ask? Its mine...

I've been screaming and reaching out

But there IS no way out

And as the days turn over and over again

It feels as though forever I'll be trapped in this prison

My own personalized hell

As I know all too well:

I'll run all I will

But can never escape myself.

MY DESIRE

Free and Fearless by *Blue-a:*

I want to go now!

Every particle of my being cries out

Or dislodge this Thorn, I'm begging, somehow

I've sought fulfillment in every place

Been left with scars that'll never erase

Unrelenting flashbacks relay the past

Taunting me with things forever passed

I've never found peace

Or a moment to believe

That my downward countenance

Shall ever be relieved

I'm dying without the Sovereign's peace

To lay down within God's fields of green

I long to walk upon those golden streets

Be forever quenched by His life-giving streams

But above all in eternity

My desire will be to throw myself on the ground

Bow at His feet

Thank Him for washing away all my Depravity

But I just want to go NOW

From this flesh finally be free
Not endure eighty years of suffering!

There is nothing left on this Earth for me
For I have tasted indeed-

All is Vanity.

LONG AGO

Desolation Dreams- Ice Lady by Suntwirl- http://suntwirl.deviantart.com/

I've always been alive

But never have I thrived

Always been just "alright"

Yet weeping within, day and night

Nope, never been able to say

That I'm even almost okay

Each day that I live

Feels like punishment

For doing the right thing

For choosing to endure the suffering

Like a sign that I should have been gone

Long, long ago.

I'm holding out though

For that one moment

I'll feel what they call "happiness"

Meanwhile, I persist to just exist

Refusing to die, even as I bleed

Like the remainder of a dying breed

Meant to perish with the foregone

And I would have been gone

Long, long ago

If I weren't so determined to see

That elusive little thing people call "Hope"

PERFECT POISON

<u>*Drowning In Sorrow*</u> *by Pure-Poison89-* <u>*http://pure-poison89.deviantart.com/*</u>

I need you in my life

It would suck without you in it

But you're my Perfect Poison

It's really quite ironic

You exude the very Drug that I've fought to get clean of

It can seem lighter when you're around

But calls my Demons to gather 'round

They whisper suggestions to me

And bitter words of jealousy

They're seeking to destroy everything

But still I can't help but compete

I hate that for which I bleed

Comes to you so easily

I need you here with me

But at the cost of much more Agony

I know I'll never behold a moment of Peace

Until I obtain that which is yours I seek

And at long last retorting

The voice of Inferiority

But in that I'm seeking a role

In which I wasn't cast

I wasn't born like you

But into a lower class

In acceptance lay the only way, I know

Despite that fact, I still can't seem to let it go

Cuz it's always right in front of me

MOCKING

Always reminding...

Of that which I desire so badly

But never will achieve

So I am left aggrieved

In this irresolvable conflict

It's all a foolish game you see

I'll lose it you can bet

But never can I embrace you...

Until I can forget

PRAYER OF PSALMS 13

My whole life I've kicked against the goads

And Your mercies You've continually shown

God, forgive me my transgressions
Each day I've my list of confessions...

But consider my sorrows!
Look upon my despair!
Number my tears!
Take into account my Suffering's years!

How Long, O Lord?
Where has Your shining countenance gone,
Of which I adored?

Have you forgotten that which Your very hand made?
With the multitude of my sorrows... How many more days?
I have no discernment, for darkness has covered my face
Rescue me my God, no longer delay!

THIS WAY

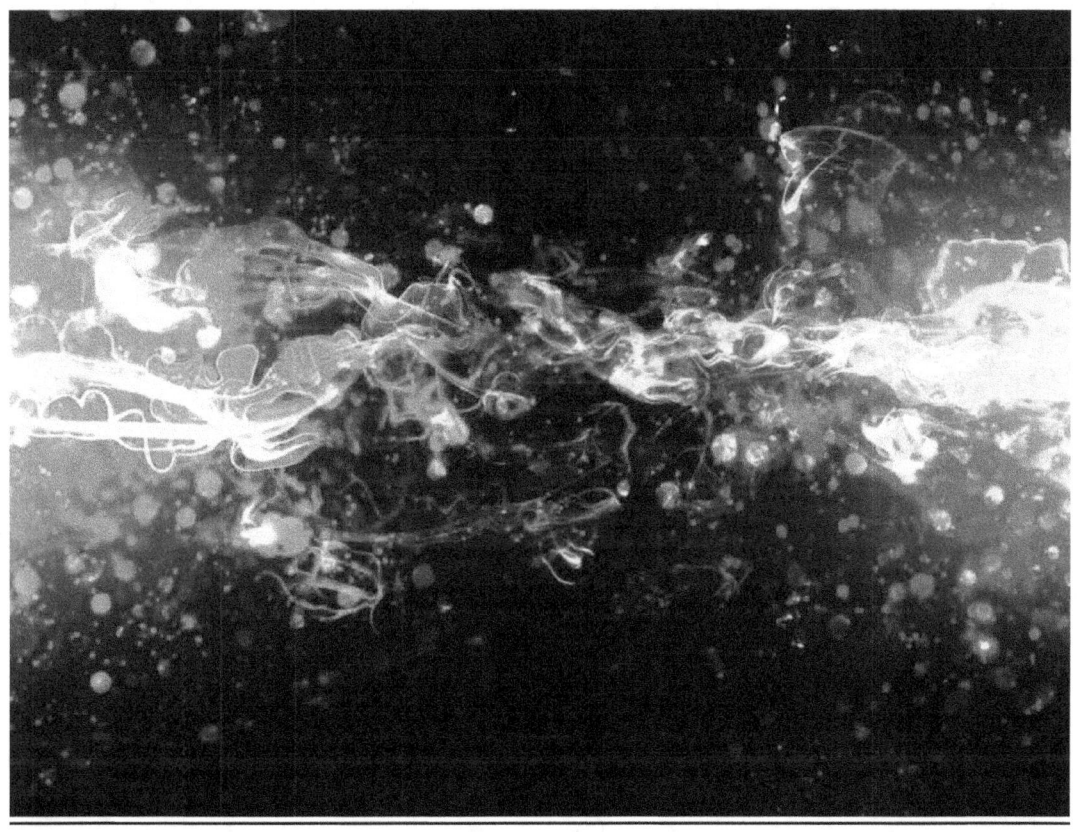

Sit quiet and listen

I'll tell you of a Way

To help you work through a life full of pain

This Way, a tool used to cope

Whilst seeking out elusive rays of hope

This Way, used to run from our fears

Grows less and less potent

With the accumulation of years

This Way of living, the strength of deprivation

Destructive as it is, a powerful consolation!

Dear small boy

This Way will work for you, now and forever!

Dear young girl

When you mature, it will grow into a fruitless endeavor

Peace to he who discovers This Way

It'll help you walk through this life full of pain

But woe to SHE who finds This Way

Seeking Its refuge in the youth of her days

She'll live Its short time

Think she'll be fine

But only delay fate

And soon shall she find

Her fears were always lurking

Only one step behind

Dear small boy

This Way will work for life

Long past when you grow up

And find a nice wife

Dear young girl

This Way will work only for a night

And leave you locked into a lifetime of fight

This Way won't bring the comfort you crave

So look elsewhere young girl

Or bow down to fate

EMPTY

Please,

I beg of Thee :

Teach me

To walk in Peace

Away from Depravity

For It dwells right within

Underneath my skin
I used to enjoy little things
But now, not for one moment

Now I have to be
Constantly running
Or the Fear following
Will overtake me

I know no one shall see what I actually mean
But maybe you can relate to the feeling empty
An emaciated soul
Only God and I can see

Please,
I beg of Thee :
Teach me
To walk in Peace
Away from Depravity

And I'll chase no one else-

No other philosophy

Nor mans foolish wisdom

Which just as soon shall cease to be

VISIONS OF A DYING WARRIOR

Die By the Sword by Blaithiel- **http://blaithiel.deviantart.com/gallery/**

You said that You would lead me

All through this life and past the end

And I wanted to follow always
My Savior, Lord, my friend

But when will You turn and see
I fell behind some time before
I'm lying back here now
Collapsed onto the floor

Have Your eyes not beheld my form
Slumped down to the ground
Now lifeless here I lie
No longer to be found

My black eyes stare vacantly
Into the fading background

No longer the eyes you knew
The ones Your hand first crafted
Setting them in blue

Don't leave me here destitute

Shrouded in solitude

Hedged in on every side,

Waiting for my own demise

Now I'm bent over the sword

-Visions of a dying Warrior

EVER LONG TIME

You've held me captive in this bind

For an ever long time

Hopelessness flooding in

Devouring my mind

You've beaten me to the ground

Anticipating that I'll bow

You've tried to break my spirit

Hoping I'll lay my weapon down

You've cast over me this veil of worthlessness

So thick I can't see past my own distress

You've driven me to the cemetery, just to wander around

And my hands hath proceeded to dig into the ground :

Digging my grave

Desperate to escape

This tortured mind depraved

All my years, You've always led me here

Whispering so persuasively,

"It's the only way to outrun your fears..."

What human mind first fathomed suicide?

Or did it crawl up from the Pit

By which I now sit?

Time and time again
You try to pull me in
By power of compulsion

But I've resisted you still-
For an Ever Long Time
Hopelessness beckoning, Gnawing at my mind

You singled me out, cut me off from my home
And now in Isolation, I contemplate tombstones

But then in the silence I heard
A Voice, but another:
A softly spoken word

And though it may take to the hour of my death
I'll seek 'til I find that Voice
To my last dying breath

BITTER GREEN

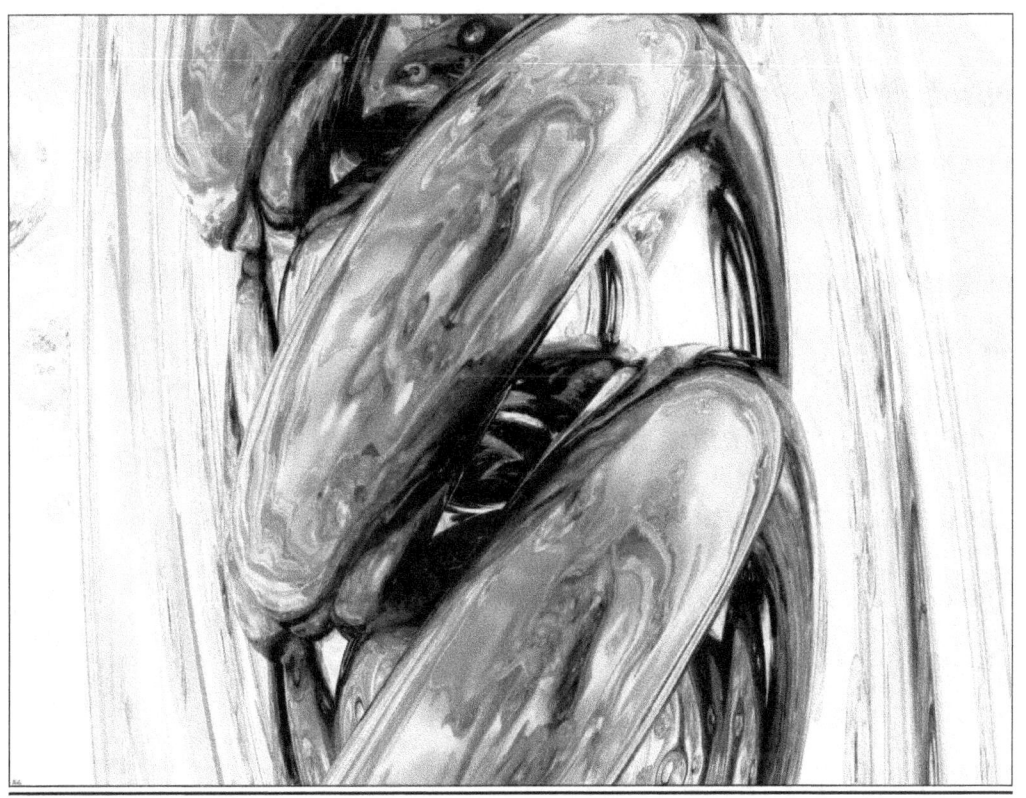

I'll Give You Some Candy by AnonymousToStrangers-
http://anonymoustostrangers.deviantart.com/

What must it be like

To have a *frickin' life

To be outside this prison cell

My personalized circle of hell

To ever smile genuinely

With no subtle Agony

Oh to stand in blissful ignorance

Enjoying all life's benefits

I keep my jaw clenched tight

For those of whom will never be required insight

Who will never know this kind of suffering

My bones break in frustration

Heart screaming with temptation

But just allow me this

For I cannot always resist :

Pour the venom in!

Overwhelmed with sin,

Sick with jealousy,

Burning with envy,

Drowning in consuming green,

Hotly resenting,

Hating unconsentedly,

Bitter as Hell ;

I may just as well

Smother my soul-

I've lost all control

It's turned light into darkness!

Good intentions to sickness!

Destroyed all my goodness!

Why!

Why!

Why?

Would it happen this way?

Oh yes - I recall:

I have to ruin everything.

WAITING 'TIL I WAKE

Straddle by EiMoOo- *http://eimooo.deviantart.com/*

I'm living in my sleep...

Waiting for this nightmare to dissipate

As if I were just anticipating
the moment I'll awake

Like one morning I'll open my eyes
And happily realize
It was all just a lie
A masochistic fabrication
Born from within my mind

And awake to a new reality
Forget the present times
Or convince myself it's all a mirage
And reality's not so unkind

That these circumstances and struggles
Will blow past me with the sands
And reveal clear skies all along
No more unquenchable demands

But the longer I look

Search and scour

To foresee my relief's hour

I lose heart

For it's all real

And my soul's hope is devoured

SOMEBODY WHISPERED TO ME

In the Middle of Nowhere (inverted)- by Pure-Poison89- http://pure-poison89.deviantart.com/

Somebody whispered to me...

"Remember who you were?

With personality?

You'd even smile sometimes

And were so much more carefree

You'd go places and do things
Cared what was happening

The person he fell in love with
The one you USED to be
Sane enough to hold his hand
And really feel something

You didn't know the cruelty
Of your current reality
Never saw it coming
Or you wouldn't have allowed his company

He's waiting around for someone
You never again shall be
So quit lying to yourself
cease pretending for him and me

We all know you'll never get better

That you've already tasted your own defeat

Haven't told him to give up yet -

But soon he too shall see

That you belong to ME

My name is Agony.

And Suffering, Depravity,

Fear, and Tragedy

Yes, you and I both know

The truth that's bound to show:

That I

Have already sucked you dry-

Right

Down

To

The

Bone.

So stop trying to fool everyone,

For you BELONG alone.

SPEAK THROUGH THE WINDS

Fade Away by Blue- a: http://blue-a.deviantart.com/gallery/

Allow me to recount the unoriginal

Expressions of a troubled individual

Tired of striving to feel happiness
When it's no longer found in the childlike kiss
My soul has naught even remembrance of it
Wishing I could sink into blissful ignorance

As much as I now understand so much more
Contentment is now all that I'm searching for
Where is it found after childhood passes?
In what venture lay the joy of satisfaction?

I need not to be told
That no sum of money
Will ever allow one to behold
A salve designed to fill
The hole within my soul

Looking to the heavens,
I feel it's there somewhere
So from my lips I raise the words,
Though tempted to doubt God cares

"I long to walk with You
To finally touch your hand
I.
AM.
SO.
TIRED.
HERE.
You alone can understand

You solely are my goodness
In You I could have no shame
I need You here beside me
To bear through all my pain

Please take it all away!
And shower me in Your grace
Deliver me from my fears
While I do not feel You near!"

May God grant me the faith to believe

He listens, answers, and oversees me.

And I'll continue to speak through the winds,

EVEN THOUGH

I hear my voice echo

REALITY AND DREAMS

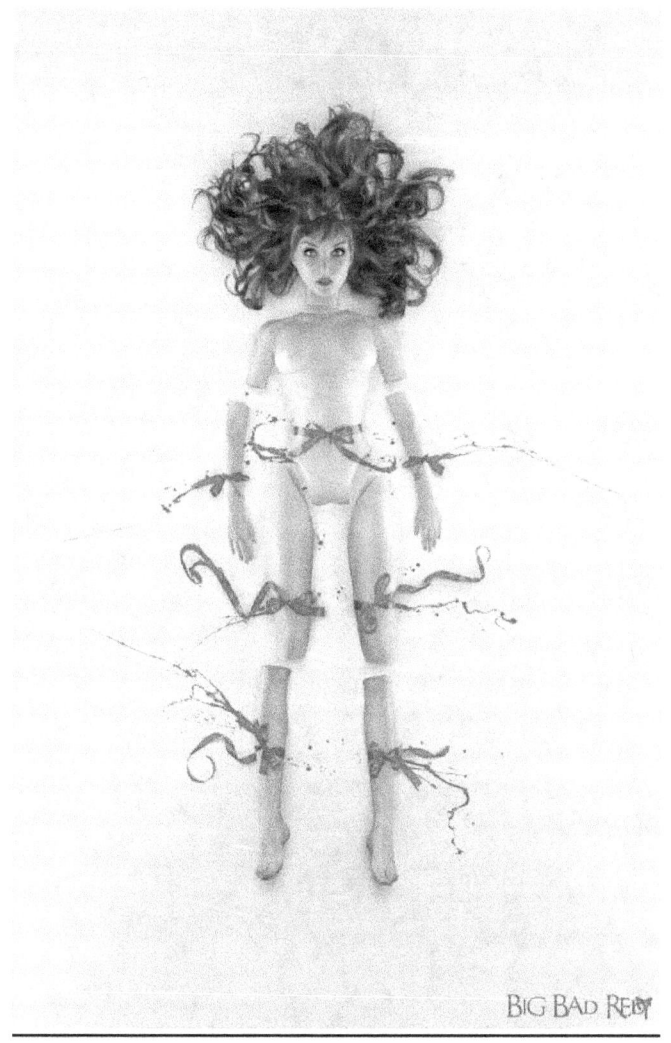

Red Ribbon by BigBad- Red- http://bigbad-red.deviantart.com/

A struggle so desperate to get out of the pit

But were so inundated within it

Open up any magazine and you shall see

Page after page of our own travesty

Guys bulk for muscle

Girls starve for bones

Perpetuating the number of idealistic clones

Measures and striving in vanity

Attain what everything says we should be

"They want a lady in the streets

And a freak in the sheets"

Yeah, thanks Ariaphoenix

I see what you mean, it's

Really a shame

To be trapped in this game

So WHAT would it mean

If you weren't the woman of his fantasies

This is reality

We have to do something differently

Cuz I can't be the only lady

Sick of chasing pipe dreams

FEAR'S MEMORIES

Feel the World by Blue-a: **http://blue-a.deviantart.com/gallery/**

I would do **anything**

Just to get rid of this thing

And think on something else

I've gone insane applying myself
To calculate a way out

'Round the clock
I gather my thoughts
To formulate new strategy.
Get up again,
Muster all strength,
And learn to be more cunning

From every angle I've aimed my tries
Contemplated a million times
But still it plays and plays
If ever this cup shall pass away
Oh that'll be the day

My Memories haunting
Ever long taunting
With better days long passed

Playing and playing

I wish they'd have stayed

Guess good things just never last

I'm trying SO HARD

But never enough it seems

The past in my mind's eye

Ever tormenting me

"Be in the moment,

Forget and move on,

Be hopeful for the future."

But my heart sings a different song

Sighing... even if I were

To get out from under

Would it be just a matter of time

'Til the struggle is again mine?

What would keep it from crawling back?

Cuz I don't even know how it happened

As though an entity has accessed the recesses of my mind

And labored to bring my hidden, unspoken fears to life

TREE OF…

Light Up by Irving GFM- http://irvinggfm.deviantart.com/

Sometimes I like to set out, just treading slowly

Only to gaze upon this one far off tree

It looks so out of place in this world of Depravity

The shade of its broad, abundant leaves

Clothed in a transcendent green-

Is Almost comforting

Like a single seed fell from heaven's garden

Just to whisper...

"Let not your hearts be hardened."

Yes maybe I'll stick around for one more day

To see if this tree

Ever blossoms even more prettily

Most reminiscence of Heaven one can find here

Intimacy with death thine eyes may endear

What I picture upon waking- when all is made clear

I'll smile conclusively

And cry my last tear

NEVER BE

These wounds... they wish

That I… could simply cease to exist

If I had just never come to be...

There would be no void,

No people I disappoint,

Nothing missing without me-

Except there'd be a bit more money

And a lot less worry

If I had just never come to be...

As it seems there's no helping me

Until God Himself chooses to intervene

But who knows if He even will?

Cuz I no longer hear His will

Taken over by all these little things

-Little I know in light of eternity

But still big enough in my reality

To be the death of me

And I see no rescuing.

If I had just never come to be...

I would never have had the opportunity

To be so selfish,

To fail at everything,

And not have enough strength

To continue in these charades.

This would never have happened

I wouldn't have had to feel the shame

Of letting you down, day after day

If you hadn't met me

No, not a single memory

If I had just never come to be...

They could have been happy.

NO MORE TIME

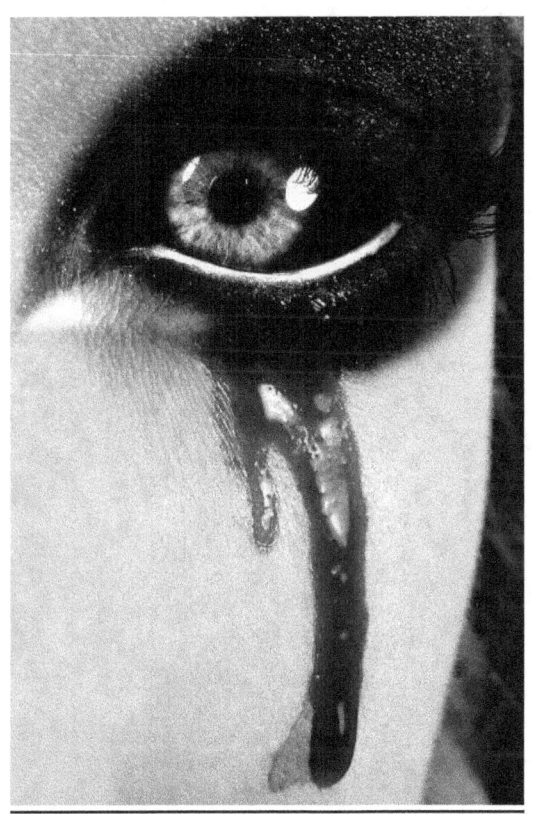

We Are Young by ObliterateOblivion-
http://obliterateoblivion.deviantart.com/

There's no more time for pleading and tears

Which fall, most apparently, on deaf ears

If rage and a cold heart will get me there-

I SWEAR

I'll become what I wasn't meant to be

To feel again like a human being

If that'll get me through-

Cuz I've been struggling

For so many years and seemingly

There's no reward for those who seek,

At the cost of their own suffering,

To honor where God placed thee

"Make due with what is given to you"

But Most days there's nothing left but judgment for me

Because I don't have the strength

And none given from Sovereignty

Despite my bleeding cries

Pathetic they are sometimes.

Go ahead and join the witch hunt-

Tell me I'm in sin

Tell me I'm in rebellion

I really never COULD win.

Worse even still-

I'm alone in this hell

Having never heard of another

No, never even met one sole other

Who's made it through this

Or can understand

And even if they did

Once experience it

They took the easy way out-

The only way out

I truly am the last of an expired breed

With no archives of such, and thus :

No solution to meet my need

PARADE

Memories by DiosaEMR- http://diosaemr.deviantart.com/gallery/

You'll just have to excuse me

For not being content with passing

My life in front of a TV screen,

To what it amounts in the scope of eternity

I can't comprehend how you don't understand

Every second ticking by

Dragging you closer to the hour you die

"Live in such a way as if it's your last day,"

We often so noncommittally say

In blind faith I once prayed

I'd endure a lifetime of pain

If only to lead one soul from the Grave

Oftentimes I wonder where all that courage went

As so most days I'm absolutely spent

Others I think myself a fool

Who spoke a word too rashly

And it wasn't worth it at all

Or maybe I should say

It isn't worth it today

I'd like to take it all back

Trade in these scars to be happy

Paste it onto my face

So I can finally join in on the parade

But I'm still just no good

(Though by now I really should)

At playing societal games

OR pretending to be sane.

CURSED- TABOO TWO

Red Ribbon2 by BigBad- Red- http://bigbad-red.deviantart.com/

Don't care who disagrees with me

As I fight for supremacy

But deep inside don't really believe

There's any advantage to being me

Every hour's striving is tiring

Just to achieve a lower degree

Of inescapable, flabby inferiority

Dont care who disagrees with me

Naught is my epitome,

Compared to that which Adam could be.

I work thrice as hard to every mean,

Burdened by physiology,

Cursed from the onset of Depravity;

It literally courses through my veins ;

Every aspect of my life pervades

Don't care who disagrees with me

I am free to repeat

That's right: I AM the weaker breed

Created to exist to fulfill a petty need

Even if they do lust and chase after me

Adam shall never know what it's like to BE

Don't care who disagrees with me

I'm going to vent unrestrainedly

And speak of what is Taboo

Now I've spelled it out so plainly for you...

What could I possibly be-

But Femininity!

Don't care who disagrees with me

I'll absolutely

Always fight Eve.

Who knows, maybe I'll come around eventually

But until then-feel trapped in the wrong body

USED TO

A Prayer For My Heart by BerryBlu- *http://berryblu.deviantart.com/*

Trying to pursue the activities

I **used to** call my hobbies

Get up to do the things I **used to**

But I'm simply no longer so easily enthused

NOTHING's what it **used to** be

What **used to** make me- me

The way **I** remember being

I'm making myself seek

that which **used to** make me happy

Even if only for a breath

Even if just for one day

But it's all just going through the motions

To **TRY** and feel emotion

I **used to** never say

"I don't know,"

But in actuality...

I'm simply lying.

*...Didn't **used to** do that either*

It's just that I don't care...

About anything

Joy, satisfaction, peace-

Naught any longer brings

Even if interest I were to feign

My efforts ever only attain

Not a damn little thing

I'd like to think there's always time for change

That it doesn't diminish to futility with age

But with every passing day

I can't tell anyway

The difference between depressed

Deathly tired, or overly stressed

The only obvious truth to see

*Is that I've lost my **FIRE,** completely:*

What **used to** make me- me
Lively, strong, spunky red- head
Eroded to dark and silent instead

And while they may say
That "She's still lovable this way"
I'm lying here wondering:
Will the Red Head's eyes ever shine again
With life in their blue
The way they **used to**?

INCORRECT EMOTION

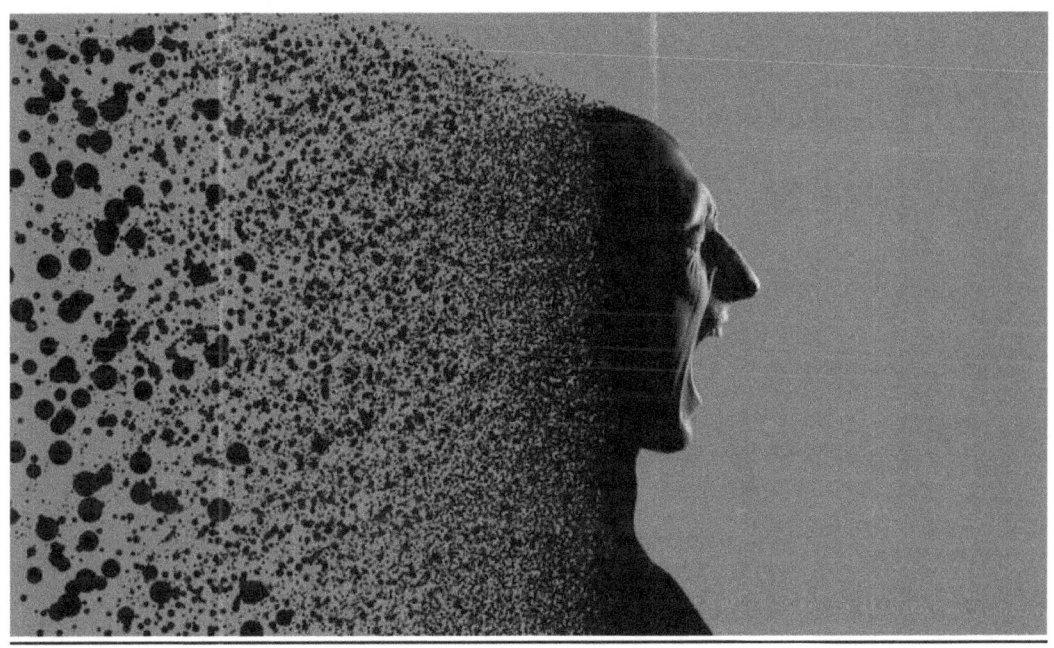

What for others happens so easily-

The way an experience is supposed to be

In circumstance which ought to make one happy

Just doesn't play out the right way for me

I now clearly see

Instinct **DOESN'T** come naturally to me

As if my own psyche

Extenuates the rest of humanity's

Don't let my meaning be misunderstood

I'd flip a switch in my mind if I could

As I HATE not feeling the way that I should

Or worse yet -

Feeling the complete opposite

I have only ever known the undesirable

And hold no power to sway my soul

Only am I acquainted- and well

To the inner conflicts stemming within ourselves

Walking through my own personal hell....

"Incorrect" emotion: only myself.

SURELY

Stop your incessant complaining!

It's driving me insane!

Nit pick at this and that

In excess of speech, where fools play

So go on and on again

Surely your voice transcends

The words of the wise

Who speak with the eyes

Assuredly you understand

All the ways of man

And you must have lived through

ALL the struggle assigned to you

So go on and on again

About all those dark places you've been

For surely your pain surpass

That of those you never asked

Protest as you will

And call me the Villain

Irregardless of such

I will say as much:

*"Oh, **DO** moan and cry*
While I keep a dry eye
I'm sorry I can't pity
'Sufferings so petty."

FINALLY

Broken by Pure-Poison89- _http://pure-poison89.deviantart.com/_

I read through your blog the other day

About all the "changes" on your road to okay

You took the easy way out

The **ONLY** way, without a doubt

But it is also Immorality's way

So In finality, you shook your fist in God's face

And never can that be erased

When its someone you'll never be able to replace

You **FINALLY** made peace with your identity

Now you're complete

You're **FINALLY**,

Exactly

What you always wanted to be

From the very beginning

And I'm just left here wondering

Where provision lay for me

Who feels the same way

yet DAILY

Still endures the suffering.
Because I choose the righteous way-
One that's paved with all the pain.

And so ascend my cries,
Every day and all night,
To God who first formed me in womb,
The way **He** saw fit to

But it's like I'm the only human being
Whose stuck in between
What I want to be
And my Destiny

So you're **FINALLY** happy...
You get to choose who to be-
While I am denied equal opportunity
Now I ask, even though selfishly:

Where's MY solution

Where's MY relief

Will someone please tell me

Where's MY FINALLY?

SPIRIT WARS

Burial Grounds by NeverDying-http://neverdying.deviantart.com/

I write not that of my own mind

But know how to listen

To the voice of the Divine

And those of different spirits

Who whisper to me in rhymes

With the same truths and lies

Existing from before time

Most of us are just mouth pieces

Used for the declarations of demons

And some of greater spirits

Warring behind the scenes

All unseen

By the souls for which they're battling

And lately, I've dissolved into silence

Because it's all the same premise.

Nothing new to see here,

All been said before.

I won't reiterate their statements

But learn to listen for something more.

FINAL DAYS

<u>Wings of Domain</u> by NeverDying-http://neverdying.deviantart.com/

We surmise that we devise our own ideations

Really we're all just empty slate creations

The spirits make us take shape

Or whittle us away

For what we will be found as on the Judgment Day

To which ones will you listen

In this invisible war of attrition?

I saw it conveyed in a dream

And I fell down on my knees

Desperately shielding my eyes

As a mighty thunder split the skies:

Torn wide open

A voice spoken

Shaking the Earth as it declared

Laying the Earth's foundations bare

East to West, a blood red sky

Stripping away all the lies,

Excuses that we hide behind,

And Idols we follow which keep us blind

The dead rose up out of their graves

Each to give account for all of his days

Some destined to die outside

The life-giving presence of the Divine

Others restored and justified

To reign with He who shall divide

Goats from the sheep

Latter: His to keep

"Woe to those who are left behind,"

The reaping angels mourn and cry,

"When Jesus returns to redeem His bride!"

I awoke petrified with dread
And heard a whisper in my head:
We need to live more urgently
To be among the dead who will ascend

So warn all you can
So their choices may be made
Lest that they should say
On the Judgement day:

"You didn't tell me!"

-But not even echoing
Across the glass sea of finality

PASSION AND TORMENT

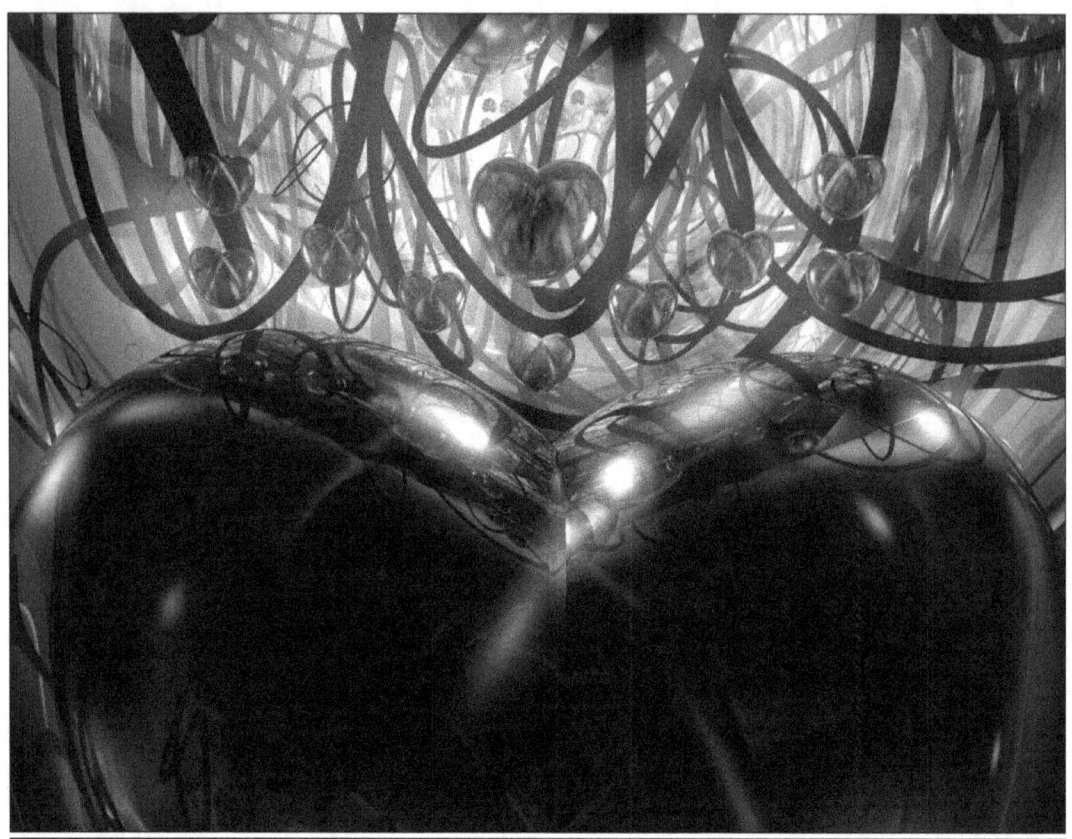

A Touch of Darkness by AnonymousToStrangers-
http://anonymoustostrangers.deviantart.com/

Now that I've tasted the forbidden fruit

I'm intoxicated- I can't forget about you

As though I've been taken by powerful drugs

This must be what it's like to have fallen in love

Yes, surely this is what everyone talks of

What they chase after, growing in obsession

Because it's absolutely beyond description

The sweet aroma of singed inhibitions

I've never felt anything even close to this

What is this feeling inside of me

Could it really be-

Actually,

Truly,

Finally:

PASSION

In me?

Like a fire burning

I can feel the heat!

And now that I've tasted- I'll have nothing less

"Lovers to the pit of hell"

But you make it sound so nice,
Your whisper so enticing

Now that you've screwed* with my mind
I find myself looking at my life
And realized just how much is missing
In just that moment we were kissing

But the darkness of this tragedy:
You only exist in my sleep.
I can only see you when I dream;
Only be near you in the deep
Trenches my soul has been building

And now I awaken
Only more lonely
For now I have truly seen
All that I'm missing

Unconscious dreams,

That turn to subconscious memories...

BLACK WIDOW

A Romance set in perversion

How can the way ever be made straight again?

"Lovers to the pit of Hell"

Like the Black Widow,

You know me too well!

Darkness lures me in

Lying in wait to destroy in the end

Oh that I could learn to desire the Light

And not be a fool to reside in the Night

But as soon as I feel what I've sought all along

-*FINALLY* something!

Turns out that it's wrong

And My Heart's breaking-

Now I'm shaking-

I can't breathe it out

'Cuz I can't go without

Take one more breath

Just one more breath

But inside my chest:

I'm so tired of this

Feelings should just come naturally

But not to me!

Why not to me?!

What spirit evil are you

That you should come seeking,

Suggesting,

Whispering,

and Tempting

Like a carrot on a string

Unconscious dreams,

That turn to Subconscious Memories :

Stop tormenting me!

You only leave me wanting

And I can never have thee

I hate myself for feeling this way

But I cannot meet you at the half way

That I may not burn on Judgement day

Lovers to the Pit of Hell :

Like the Black Widow,

You know me too well!

But still-

Now you've just wrecked me

And simply ruined everything!

MORTALITY'S BIND

Trapped in humanity's bind-

To leave the pain behind

Half of me must die

Or be forever trapped in between

For the length of my stay in mortality

I'm sorry I can't sit next to you

Without doing what I have to

I'm sorry that everyone hates me

For being what I have to be

But at some point I simply have to let go

Cuz I cannot keep up with this exhausting show

I've been there and back

This is the only way- I know

As soon as I experience a moment of peace

As I feel for a second what it is to be

Again me-

A taste so sweet

As soon as just a moment so fleeting

Finally settles, gracing upon me

Surely I'm shoved again underneath

To remain crushed by the yoke of my Agony

And now I am speechless

Cuz now I have seen

No way of escaping,

There's no help for me

NOT TIME

Blue Sea by Barbara Florczyk, Kokoszkaa-

http://kokoszkaa.deviantart.com/gallery/

I sure feel like I have no place

-Just taking up space

But it's always been hard

So please disregard

The tears streaming down my face

Gotta step up

Even though I've had enough

The ground won't move for me

Gotta just keep swimming

-Just like Dory

But make no mistake,

I've had more than I can take.

Don't wanna be standing here,

But I won't seem to disappear.

So there's just something in my eye,

Cuz I've used up all my time to cry.

It's not my time to die,

Though I may feel like it inside.

COUNTDOWN

Graviton by ErikShoemaker-_http://erikshoemaker.deviantart.com/gallery/

It's coming-

Mortality is closing.

The end hangs thick in the air,

As the smell is wafting up

Of our rebellion and despair

Bigger than them, you, or I.

Greater than all for which we've strived:

Make way for the Holy one

Holding all power over Earth, Moon, and Sun

Judgment will be done

Or salvation won

By He who is to come-

Exempt is no one

Fear and tremble

At the four horsemen

Handed the keys

To Death and Hades,

Given all authority

All permit to destroy.

Mankind's wickedness

Shall now take its toll

-Paid in full

No escape for them, you, nor I

This is the final countdown

To the coming blood red sky

PLAY DEAD

Wish I knew how

To play dead.

It won't get out
Of my head

It's eating me
From inside out
Wish I knew how
To play dead.
So maybe then
It'd flee my presence.

I'll lay there in peace
Won't even breathe,
I promise

I'll lay so very still
Lungs will not fill,
Nail in my coffin
So my heart can heal

Meanwhile

I'll contemplate escape

From this dark place,

Pale faced

Wish I knew how

To play dead

Get out of my head

Finally find some rest

I need hope.

The elegant words are gone.

I need hope.

Til then,

Like I said:

I'll simply

Learn to play dead

MEMORIES

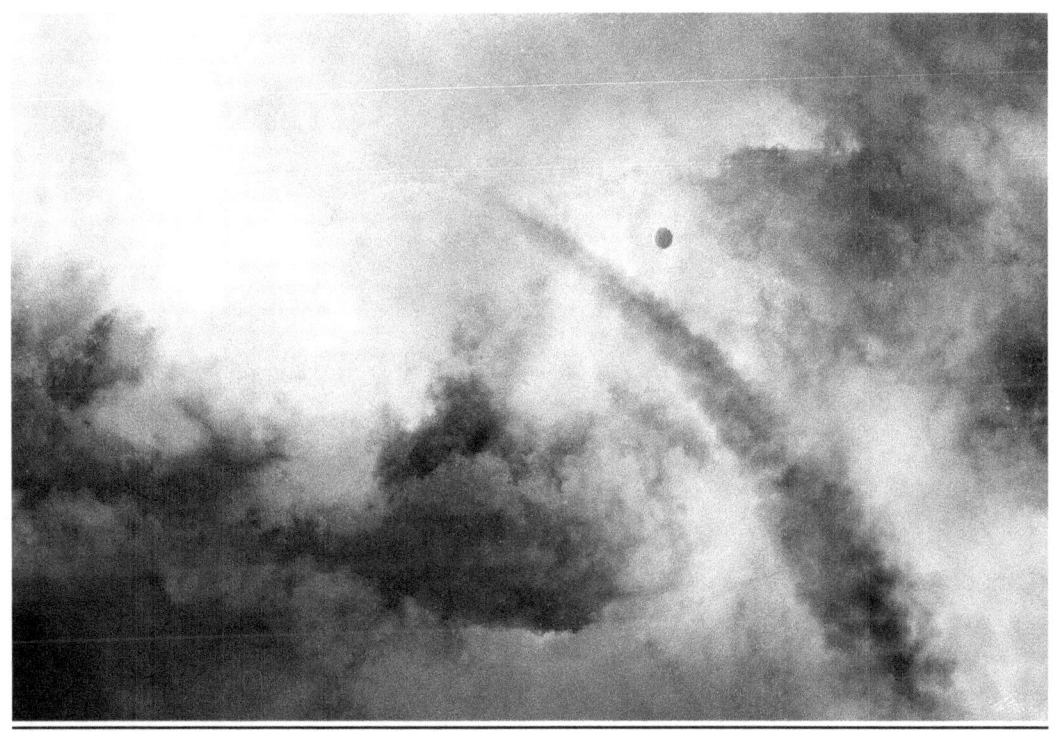

Auf Dem Nevelmeer by ErikShoemaker-

http://erikshoemaker.deviantart.com/gallery/

Memories

In the night illuminating

Cease

Tor-

Ture-

Ing

Me.

Memories

In the night illuminating

Only I can see

What haunts my subconscious memories

In each night's dreams

I hate this

I hate me

I hate them- for not leaving

I'll get away

That I will, one day…

So I fell in love

With the wrong one

Now all that's left of you

Are these infernal memories

In the night illuminating

Haunt-

ing

Me

I really am glad to see

That you're happy

But now love to me

Is just an untamed Beast

It never works, you see

And is only very frustrating.

Dreams,

Feeling,

Passion,

Love,

All of the above

Are memories

Illuminating

Killing me slowly

Leave me be...

Cease

Tor-

Men-

Ting

Me!

FORCED FORFEIT

The Mind of a Dreamer by *Blue- a:* http://blue-a.deviantart.com/gallery/

My face buried in the ground

Darkness growing around

My hope has been deferred
My cries were not heard

I was dragged,
Drugged, and tricked
Fate sure is sick.

I was chained to this chair
To sit and stare,
Hatefully glare
At my worst fear

Now here he stands
Making his demands
Spitting in my face
Laughing and replaying
All my attempts at escape
Cuz I thought that I had
Outsmarted fate

He now gloatingly restates
All the things I had said
Like I'd never come back again
And returning was not an option

-Not alive

And though the sun still shines
It's only dark and dead inside.

My season is past its prime
Now it is time
To jump off the cliff
– a forced forfeit
I HATE THIS.

FORSAKEN PLACES

Magic Tree by by Barbara Florczyk, Kokoszkaa-
http://kokoszkaa.deviantart.com/

Reality's no longer so real you see

Day by day

It's dissipating

Slowly fading away

Into another Forsaken Place

With each night, as darkness sets in
The mind escapes from its prison-
Call it a coping mechanism.
Slipping away from this Forsaken Place
To the world within it has fabricated

But curse the rising sun
Resurrecting on and on,
Drawing out from sleep,
Dissolving dreams,
Awaking with each morning
Depression's anxieties

"Why won't you let me stay?"
-Not having the strength for one more day
But only for Pretending- oh come now, let's play
Coloring a palatable fantasy
Where reality's on pause
And we're no longer lost

So don't worry about me,

As long as I sleep

The pain is erased

In the safest of havens

Shutout, frozen over…

No more Forsaken Places

PRAYER FOR TODAY

<u>Angel's Breathe</u> by DiosaEMR- **http://diosaemr.deviantart.com/gallery/**

Lord You have seen each of my days,

More familiar than I with all of my ways

You alone know why I do as I do,

Before time began my struggles foreknew

I want to believe that You are here with me

Your invisible hand guiding, protecting.

But the thousands of days

In this place I have lain

Sure feel today to have all been in vain

Please show me the way

Cuz I've been blinded by pain,

And aware I cannot see clear,

For myself hold disdain

Lift this depression,

Free my anxieties,

Rain your peace in this season,

And enlighten my eyes to see

I'm needing a reason to get up in the morning

To speak out above this Thorn I am bearing

And none of my companions can understand why

As none them feel what I do each day I'm alive

These are my supplications I make with thanksgiving

Breath by breath, Jesus, help me with living

Strengthen me for something of meaning this day

That remains in Your sight when I pass away

TRULY- Matthew 7:21-23

Where Is The Faith by IrvingGFM- http://irvinggfm.deviantart.com/

"Do you really know what it means to follow me?

Are you truly willing to give up everything?

Though I called and beckoned softly

You never turned in answering

Or you claimed My name

But of it not a thing you'd say

Where you lived or in your workplace.

You were sure every Sunday to sit in the pew

But who I Am, you never truly knew.

You'd sit down to pray

When you needed something

And ONLY THEN,

But still dared call Me your friend

I wanted to listen, comfort, and give instruction

But your own image of Me you'd already constructed

As long as it suits your needs, you're willing to follow Me

But for you alone, I gave up everything

Hear me-

I'm beckoning you to turn and see

That I NEVER KNEW YOU truly,

And you do not know Me

And truly to you I say this one thing only:

Die to self,

Pick up your cross,

And truly follow Me"

IDENTITY'S WORTH

Pull Me Down by Barbara Florczyk, Kokoszkaa-
http://kokoszkaa.deviantart.com/

Be careful what you place your identity in

It could all be taken away in just a single moment

-And likely indeed.

Be wary what you base your worth in

Cuz it aint gonna last in the end,

Model, athlete, artist

Stoner, sinner, saint

Even most perfect of vessels surely shall grow tainted.

And just when you think you know yourself,

It all slips away when you go through hell

The torturous window of retrospect -beware

For the day will come you'll have to sit there

And stay like a cripple, staring out that window.

By sickness or death, you shall be brought low.

But how would I know…?

Cuz I've been there,

And for a number of years-

It's been the hardest pill I've ever had to swallow.

And though a simple, common rhyme:

It's left me perfectly hollow,

In Christ alone.

Or at least they say so.

Stripped of every identity,

And now I'm nothing

But covered in mercy

God knows: I need plenty.

But how can one make right of so much pain

How can I rectify so much suffering?

More so still,

Why won't God simply take it away?

Probably to teach SO MANY ONE THING:

That God loves despite- everything we fight

And each of us He loves

Even when there's nothing that we're capable of.

ABOUT BLOODY ENDURANCE

This collection of poems was written for the purpose of giving a voice to those enduring various sorrows and struggles. Written over the course of the hardest year (thus far) of my life- each poem is of a chronological, very specific, storytelling nature. However, details were omitted in order to give each individual reader creative license to interpret as they please- according to their own experiences. By no means was this book written with the intent to perpetuate or glorify darkness. This was done to provide the small amount of solace that may come in times of suffering through the means of expression, allowing one to know that others can relate and have also walked through (and perhaps conquered) such darkness. Hold strong: readers, hold hope: those who mourn, and hold fast to Christ: all.

-Endurance Warrior

"Teaching them to observe all things that I have commanded you; and lo, I am with you always, even to the end of the age." Amen.

Matthew 28:20

A NOTE ABOUT

Expressions of Agony-

This was the very first thing I had written in many years. It started out as a journal entry, but when sentences fell flat to express what I wanted to convey, I found that outlet by poetry. With uncensored, true expressions of a troubled spirit, this first touches on the backlash of living in a fallen world afflicted and influenced by demonic/angelic forces. And thus Agony (and various other un-emerged representations) is addressed as a personified entity. For those in the deepest pits of depression, it is so literally a battle of bloody endurance to maintain normalcy of life functioning and interest in any activity, when all desired is the end of the struggle (and in that mind state- life). At times, life can then feel like a tiresome imposition.

Puppet

As humans, are we really born with instinct? Or are we molded and formed by what we are taught to perceive? Does original thought REALLY exist or are we humans only vessels through which spirits can act out and express themselves? If we did have our own mind, would we recognize thoughts that did not originate within us? Where then do they come from?

Each thought to enter the human mind should be interpreted as to its source and then determined valid or not. Again emphasizing the human struggle expressed in **Ephesians 6:12**.

> "For we do not wrestle against flesh and blood, but against the rulers, against the authorities, against the cosmic powers over this present darkness, against the spiritual forces of evil in the heavenly places. "

Again, this is not an easy struggle and can mean a life time of "warfare." But it is the battle for your mind…and ultimately, your soul.

Time's Ritual

Doesn't life sometimes feel like one giant monotonous, inescapable, ritual? The very act of being born demands that humankind work itself back into the dust from whence it came. Simply existing, we have needs that must be worked for (food, shelter, health, wants- by means of typically non-optional schooling and careers). Also, most people don't savor the thought of growing old, but it's sure coming just as fast anyways, huh? Meanwhile, let us ever keep the concept of time in mind. For one should use the length of life allotted to him for a purpose that will remain after his passing. I'll keep reminding myself too.

Once Again

This is about the times that we give our best to accomplish, change, or bring about a certain results in our lives- only to end up feeling weak and faced with our own Depravity.

Truly nothing of lasting value can be accomplished without the help and/or rescue of God. Especially in the area of overcoming each of our own personal demons, I have often found all the strength I have to give, insufficient. As if the harder I try on my own strength, the more frustrated I feel by getting nowhere as time goes by. By painful trial and error…I know 2 Corinthians 12:8-9 and Philippians 4:13 are so inescapably true:

2 Corinthians 12:8–9

"Three times I pleaded with the Lord about this, that it should leave me. But he said to me, "My grace is sufficient for you, for My power is made perfect in weakness. Therefore, I will boast all the more gladly of my weaknesses, so that the power of Christ may rest upon me."

Philippians 4:13

"I can do all things through Christ who strengthens me."

Target Point

FIGHT! FIGHT! FIGHT! NEVER, NEVER, NEVER GIVE UP! Even if everyone around you AND (especially) inside you tells you it's hopeless, there is no other option than to keep trying, now is there? Whatever "IT" may be for you personally, recognize that others' fate is not yours. It does not have to be yours and you CAN be the exception. There are so many forces out to oppose us, so don't lose your fight!

1 Peter 5:8

"Be sober, be vigilant; because your adversary the devil walks about like a roaring lion, seeking whom he may devour."

Fake Paths

Worn, tired, and sick; a cry of exhausted striving, loneliness, futility, and a cracked smiling mask.

Take It Away

Pleading prayer for encouragement and strength to walk one more day.

No Longer

It would be wise to never cast judgment or condemnation upon another... For you never know what you may soon experience yourself. Anytime, anyone, anything. I myself have had extensive dreams in which I experienced a wide array of anguishes brought about by various troubles- in fact, this was written in the waking space between dreams one night. Most of the experiences, dreams, and issues I have faced I had long (subconsciously) assumed that I would never be able to identify with. Life is ironic like that.

Dear Fear

A sweet little letter written to the personified entity of Fear.

Bleed

When everyone thinks that they know better: what is best for you; except you of course. Sometimes peoples' best intentions only hurt us in the end.

Go Ahead

This is about being forced into situations that are completely out of your control. When you feel so powerless but are still determined to stand... Lock and load! Gear up for war, from the inside out! In the end, no one can take away your spirit, or what makes you- you.

I Wept

I wrote this about how difference of perspective or opinions can drive people apart- especially when one chooses a different path than that which others feel they should go. Unfortunately, conflicts cannot always be resolved.

Sheol's Souls

Every human being has turned away from God in futile wickedness:

Isaiah 53:6

All we like sheep have gone astray;
We have turned, every one, to his own way;
And the LORD has laid on Him the iniquity of us all.

Romans 3:10-12

"As it is written:

'There is none righteous, no, not one;
There is none who understands;
There is none who seeks after God.
¹² They have all turned aside;
They have together become unprofitable;
There is none who does good, no, not one.'"

Good thing God paid the 'ransom' to give our spirit and soul the opportunity to pass on into life, instead of to the depths of Sheol- eternal death. But you must make a choice to commit your already enslaved soul to a different owner.

Leave

This speaks of the process of grieving when you lose someone you love (by death, separation, misunderstanding, conflict, or other means).

Especially for someone who has experienced loss over and over again… They may not necessarily desire yet another companion, which would open them up for the potential of more loss, even if good-intentioned people seek to help or comfort them.

Tide's Time

When you've done all you can and it's just not enough…STAND. When all that's left is to face your worst fear….BE STRONG.

It Beats

I was wondering just how much and for how long one can endure such depths of pain and sorrow in a depression seemingly endless and absolutely isolating.

Proverbs 13:12

12 Hope deferred makes the heart sick,
but a desire fulfilled is a tree of life.

A difficult decision to be made in the midst of any struggle is to allow it to shape one's character. There is something to be said for being one familiar with suffering- as those are the people most qualified to help and support those who will walk through those valleys at a later time. Even if no solution can be offered for struggles, there can be comfort in knowing that someone else has already gone down the very road that we are stumbling upon. Those in the midst of incredible pain and sorrows: hold fast and know that there are those who have gone before! While this applies to those around us, Jesus Christ is one who has suffered much, understands completely, and sympathizes with you in every struggle!

Isaiah 53

"He was a man of sorrows and acquainted with grief."

Hebrews 4:15

"For we do not have a high priest who is unable to sympathize with our weaknesses, but one who in every respect has been tempted as we are, yet without sin."

I have found that God allows even His children to suffer a great range of things so that they may later help others in the specific burdens appointed to them. Never were any promises made that life would be easy (as cliché as I know that sounds), but we are called to "**Bear one another's burdens, and so fulfill the law of Christ (Galatians 6:2)**"

Romans 5:3-4

"Not only that, but we rejoice in our sufferings, knowing that suffering produces endurance, and endurance produces character, and character produces hope."

And yet…easier said than done.

Who I Was

After running into an old friend, some years down the road at which we parted ways, I was reflecting upon the person I was back then. Life often takes us down unexpected, twisted paths.

One Night In My Nightmares

Simply awakening with a nightmare, and turning to write it down. Though at the risk of nauseating some, it IS about vampires- of a formerly docile nature, forsaking such.

The Culmination

I'm just waiting for the day when all will be revealed, and all the suffering…will make sense.

Romans 8:28
"And we know that all things work together for good to those who love God, to those who are the called according to His purpose."

Winds

This was written of when life seems circular, purposeless, or without meaning… Most of the book of Ecclesiastes covers the concept, most specifically chapter one.

Ecclesiastes 1:1-11

"The words of the Preacher, the son of David, king in
Jerusalem.

2 'Vanity of vanities,' says the Preacher;
'Vanity of vanities, all is vanity.

3 What profit has a man from all his labor
In which he toils under the sun?
4 One generation passes away, and another generation comes;
But the earth abides forever.
5 The sun also rises, and the sun goes down,
And hastens to the place where it arose.
6 The wind goes toward the south,
And turns around to the north;
The wind whirls about continually,
And comes again on its circuit.
7 All the rivers run into the sea,
Yet the sea is not full;
To the place from which the rivers come,
There they return again.
8 All things are full of labor;
Man cannot express it.
The eye is not satisfied with seeing,
Nor the ear filled with hearing.

9 That which has been is what will be,
That which is done is what will be done,
And there is nothing new under the sun.
10 Is there anything of which it may be said,
"See, this is new"?
It has already been in ancient times before us.

[11] There is no remembrance of former things,
Nor will there be any remembrance of things that are to come
By those who will come after.'"

Wounds- I Wish

For those who struggle with self injury… Sometimes there
are simply no words strong enough

This Is Me

Most every heart has its darkness. Some live their entire
lives

terrified of allowing others to see their failures and
imperfections.

So let's just skip all the formalities

And you can decide

If you want to know me

Peace In Death

Life is a journey and death is the sure destination. The time in between is a matter of what you will do with it, what will last after your passing, and how you will face death without fear. So, are you confident about what's on the other side?

Oh how sweet be the yearning

For Death's tide of turning

Trapped

Was written about chronic, unrelenting, inescapable, inexplicable anxieties.

My Desire

This poem expresses desire to pass on into eternity and experience new life, as well as a longing for the return of Jesus Christ.

Romans 8:19-23

"[19] For the earnest expectation of the creation eagerly waits for the revealing of the sons of God. [20] For the creation was subjected to futility, not willingly, but because of Him who subjected it in hope; [21] because the creation itself also will be delivered from the bondage of corruption into the glorious liberty of the children of God. [22] For we know that the whole creation groans and labors with birth pangs together until now. [23] Not only that, but we also who have the first fruits of the Spirit, even we ourselves groan within ourselves, eagerly waiting for the adoption, the redemption of our body. "

Long Ago

Waiting.

Waiting,

Waiting,

So painfully,

So long,

So very hopelessly...

For a better day...

Or the passing away...

Of all the pain.

Perfect Poison

Sometimes the best things for us can also be the worst, when our sin nature twists and distorts that first meant for good.

This Way

This is about the societal, physiological, and emotional differences between the sexes.

Empty

Is about confessing complete depravity and inability to bring about change in one's own life by surrendering and acknowledging that all knowledge, wisdom, and power is possessed by God alone.

Visions of a Dying Warrior

Is about feeling as though God has forsaken or forgotten you, and that no help is coming in your most dire of hours.

Deuteronomy 31:6
Be strong and courageous. Do not be afraid or terrified because of them, for the LORD your God goes with you; he will never leave you nor forsake you."

Ever Long Time

Is of tirelessly clawing through the darkness- though it may have the best of you for now- until one can catch sight of Hope.

Bitter Green

Jealousy, even when one recognizes it as wrong, grows to bitterness and resentment- and destroys every good thing in the end.

Waiting 'Til I Wake

Is about waking up each day with the pointed intention to make it a better one, yet failing with each and every day. Eventually one can cope by rejecting reality, as in the case of a depressed person sleeping a lot. Or the depressed person's mind can cope with chronic emotional or physical pain by fabricating an alternate reality in their dreaming (sleeping) hours. Once this other "life" has been established, it comparatively creates an intensified disappointment with real life upon awakening each morning.

Somebody Whispered to Me

The dialogue within the recesses of our mind.

Speak Through the Wind

Was written to encourage prayer even when you don't believe God is listening any more (or ever was). It is of choosing to continue to petition- despite hearing nothing but the winds and your own voice, echoing back to your ears and heart.

At some point one will find that when childlike bliss, ignorance, and ease of amusement pass; all can feel rather empty, meaningless, or futile...as is addressed in the book of Ecclesiastes- a book of wisdom indeed!

Fear's Memories

The fear of past circumstance and struggles coming back again- outside of one's control; as well as the fear of never overcoming current obstacles or facing down one's demons to defeat.

Tree Of...

Pressing on in a world of sorrow in holding hopes of a new Heaven and new Earth. **Revelation Ch. 21**

Never Be

At the epitome of frustration and discouragement, I have often felt as though I would prefer to have never existed in the first place- seemingly saving many the trouble.

No More Time

Was written of feeling absolutely, devastatingly tired and alone in a situation you are convinced no others have a true solution to- just

Band-Aids and more strength of will. Feeling as if you have done all you can muster and have lost hope, a heart can turn bitter and cold.

Parade

Is about recalling having prayed as a child that I would suffer whatever was necessary to bring even one person to Christ's salvation- I sometimes question my judgment in the midst of pain.

Used To

Mourning the loss of oneself.

Incorrect Emotion

Do you ever feel like you're the only one that the laws of the universe (the positive aspects of) extenuate? Or that your own mind works differently than everyone else, to an infuriating degree?

Surely

An ironic vent- being at your wits end with peoples' unnecessary quarreling and complaining.

Finally

Was written about hearing and reading stories of people in your position who find their solution- whether by luck or by means of sin.

Spirit Wars

A period of long silence in my writing with no new inspired thoughts.

Final Days

Recounting a dream I had.

Not Time

Written about clenching your jaw and going about the daily routine- through all the motions- ignoring one's own tears.

Countdown

Just more visions of the end of the world and stuff.

Play Dead

The concept of "playing dead" so that one's torment(ors) will depart.

Memories

Is about countless memories in haunting flashbacks. Sometimes a good memory is a terrible thing to have.

Forced Forfeit

Is of when the fears you have been only running from finally catch up to you.

About the Author: Simply one familiar with suffering, using the pen to speak for all despair.

-The Endurance Warrior